"We can all relate to feeling o\[verwhelmed...\] has put thoughts and Scriptur\[e...\] from focusing on your circumstances and what this world has to offer to the secret place where true joy is found – in God and His Word. In the pages of this book, you'll find encouragement to keep your eyes fixed on the One who holds you through every season of life until the end. You will discover who God is and learn how to apply all He has for you to your everyday life. There are many devotionals out there, but this one delivers the goods in a biblically-based way that will bring you into the very presence of God each day."
-*Lisa Hibbs (Pastor's wife of Calvary Chapel Chino Hills)*

"I think most of us, if not all of us, want to grow in our prayer life. Christy's book, Magnify! doesn't just tell us what we should do. Christy teaches us how. In just a few minutes a day, her book gives soul nourishing truth we can apply throughout the day.
In a time where my attention is pulled in a million directions, this book is helping me gain lost ground. What treasures are in these pages. I am so grateful for this book!"
-*Sherri Youngward (Christian singer and songwriter)*

"Christy's intense love for Jesus shines through in her writing. She has a gift of inspiring you to draw closer to Jesus. As you read each daily chapter, you'll feel encouraged to completely surrender every part of your life to Jesus."
-*Patricia Apple (Pastor's wife of Calvary Chapel Tel Aviv/ The Shepherd's Light)*

"There are many voices around us shouting for us to listen. This can leave us confused, frustrated, and afraid. I've watched Christy Duff walk through storms and complicated situations. Having three teenagers and a busy husband certainly requires keeping your eyes on True North, your feet on solid ground, and having a first love for God and His Word. I'm excited for you to hold this book in your hands and be encouraged by God as you glean from the lessons that Christy has not only learned but applied."
Debbi Bryson (Speaker and Author)

"To magnify means to make (something) appear larger than it is, especially with a lens or microscope. Magnify takes us on a journey in which we daily discover the keys to exalting and glorifying God through the lens of scripture as truth is revealed and God's character is knit within our hearts and minds. In this insightful devotional, Christy leads us into a clear focus of the vastness and greatness of our Holy and Righteous God, while inspiring us to a deeper and more devoted worship of Him."
-*Brenda Leavenworth (Pastor's wife of Reliance Church)*

"I love this book. Magnify! Is an invitation to intimacy with the same Father who silences heaven to listen to the prayers of the saints. This book is an ardent call to remember the God who bends down to listen when His children magnify His name. This is an opportunity to set our hearts ablaze for such a time as this. Thank you, Christy, for such a timely book, and a great discipleship tool as well!"
-*Mercedes Miller (Pastor's wife of Calvary Chapel Grapevine)*

Magnify!

A Thirty Day Practice of Bending Down to Look Up

Christy Duff

Magnify!
A Thirty Day Practice of Bending Down to Look Up

Copyright © by Christy Duff

All rights reserved. No part of this publication may be reproduced, stored in a retrieval system, or transmitted in any form by any means, electronic, mechanical, photocopy, recording, or otherwise, without the prior permission of the publisher, except as provided by USA copyright law.

First printing, 2020

All Scripture quotations in this book, unless otherwise indicated, are taken from the New King James Version. Copyright © 1982 by Thomas Nelson. Used by permission. All rights reserved.

Scripture quotations marked NLT are taken from the Holy Bible, New Living Translation, copyright © 1966, 2004, 2015 by Tyndale House Foundation. Used by permission of Tyndale House Publishers, a Division of Tyndale House Ministries, Carol Stream, Illinois 60189. All rights reserved.

Scripture quotations marked (AMP) are taken from the Amplified Bible, Copyright © 1954, 1958, 1962, 1964, 1965, 1978 by the Lockman Foundation. Used by permission.

Scripture quotations marked NIV are taken from the Holy Bible, New International Version, ® NIV® Copyright © 1973, 1978, 1984, 2011 by Biblica, Inc. ™ Used by permission of Zondervan. All rights reserved worldwide. www.zondervan.com. The "NIV" and "New International Version are trademarks registered in the United States Patent and Trademark Office by Biblica, Inc ®

Scripture quotations taken from the New American Standard ® (NASB), Copyright © 1960, 1962, 1963, 1968, 1971, 1972, 1973, 1975, 1977, 1995 by the Lockman Foundation Used by permission. www.Lockman.org

Magnify!

To my Jesus who gave me the words to say...

To my amazing husband who kept me supplied with cappuccinos...

To my ever-patient kids who kept the house quiet(ish)
so that I could write...

Magnify!

"I bow down toward your Holy Temple and give thanks to your name for your steadfast love and your faithfulness, for you have exalted above all things your name and your Word. On the day I called, you answered me; my strength of soul you increased."
Psalm 138:2-3 (ESV)

Dear beautiful friend,

My prayer for you as we travel through this book together is that by bending low a few times a day, a greater perspective of our awesome God will be gained. Though the LORD is high, He regards the lowly. (Psalm 138:6) What a marvelous thing it is that the God of all the earth would bend His ear close to hear our prayers. That truth makes me want to be a woman who regularly moves mountains while praying! That truth makes me want to be one who has a heart and mind that prays without ceasing; ever lifting up His glorious name and bringing praise before His throne for His faithful ways and steadfast love. My prayer is that this thirty-day prayer habit will leave us filled with less of ourselves, and filled instead with a greater awe of God, a greater appreciation of who He is, and a greater understanding of who He wants to be in our lives. My prayer is that, whether for the first time or once again, this book will be used to raise up within us a passionate desire to be mighty prayer warriors for the Kingdom of God. With our hearts focused daily on an attribute of God, with our minds meditating upon verses about His greatness, and a daily listing of all that we're thankful for, how could our hearts not be elevated to His throne room and changed forever?

The steadfast love of the Lord endures forever. His ear is ever open to our cries. He is mighty, and His ways are high above our own. I pray that we will be fully immersed in His character, more and more each day, until He finally calls us home to His Kingdom that He has created us to dwell in together for all of eternity. I pray that this book would be used to help steady our gaze upon Jesus, with eyes wide open to His love, fixed upon His face, and with hearts growing closer to Him each day. Ready?

Love, Christy

Magnify!

Getting Started

When I was a little girl I loved going to Fresno, California to visit my great grandma, Lucie. I would lie for what felt like hours on her green shag carpet and look up at her as she sat at her desk and read her books. Now, as an adult, there's a piece of me that looks back at little me in my memory and wants to yell, "GET UP! How often do you think a ninety-two-year-old woman can vacuum and clean a green shag carpet?!" Ha! But mostly I think back to that time and remember how I loved laying down and looking up at her as she read because she had a giant magnifying glass that was clamped to the side of her desk, and it made her eyes look hilariously huge! I would lay there and giggle at the way the magnifying glass changed the shape of her face and her eyes, all because of my perspective from the ground, looking up.

Similarly, we view life from different angles. Magnification in our sight and thoughts depends on the perspective with which we view life. Sometimes we unintentionally magnify that which was created to be small in our thoughts, while forgetting to intentionally magnify the things in life that are worthy of magnification, like God and His vast awesomeness!

We naturally magnify that which we think of often, and there are many things in this life and world that can be magnified by our thoughts. We can magnify health problems, financial problems, marriage problems, single person problems, childrearing problems, house or car problems, or problems with the lack thereof! The list of problems we often magnify could go on and on and on and on. We unintentionally magnify the things of this world and this life by letting our thoughts dwell down here below. How much better to instead choose to live life magnifying our beautiful God! We can choose to have thoughts that are intentionally placed upon Him and His sovereignty, His goodness, His love, His mercy, His joy for us, His kindness, His grace, His hope that He brings to us; and that glorious list could go on and on and on as well.

I think the question we need to ask ourselves often should be, "What will I choose to magnify right now?" What will we choose to 'look' at with our thoughts? What will we choose to dwell on with our minds? Colossians 3:2 says, **"Set your mind on things above, not on things on the earth."** Setting our minds on things of the earth is to magnify in our thoughts those things that are passing away; those things that are earthly; those things that are worrisome, troublesome, and not worthy of our attention. But setting our minds on things above is to magnify our God in the beauty of His Holiness, in the lavishness of His love, in the wonder of His grace, and in His sacrifice upon the cross. We can also go on and on and on with our thoughts set on the list of the worthy things from above, magnifying the attributes of God that will set our minds at ease and fill us with incomparable peace and joy.

I remember the day that God caused Daniel chapter 6 to jump out to my heart in a huge way. You know how you can read a chapter of the Bible and have many things stick out to you, but there's just some days where God seems to have the words jump right off of the page as if they were written just for you, just for this moment? This was one of those days. Our whole family was in a hotel room on our way home from Thanksgiving with relatives, and I was up before them spending time with Jesus in front of a big, chilly window, reading the book of Daniel. Maybe you know his story, maybe you don't. Feel free to put this book down and go read his God-breathed story instead! But in case you want to keep reading here, I'll go ahead and give you the abbreviated version of his life. Babylon invaded Israel in the year 605 B.C. and King Nebuchadnezzar had many Israelite boys brought into his kingdom to become eunuchs in his palace and to learn the Babylonian way. Their names were changed, their lives had changed, the pressures of the culture had changed; everything that they knew and loved had changed! Despite the fact that there were no more godly influences upon their lives, there were a few boys who chose not to change along with all of the newness they were being pressured to conform to. Daniel was one of these boys. Daniel chose to continue to love the LORD God with all of his heart, soul, mind, and strength. He chose to still serve His God with his life, and to turn away from the carnal passions he saw in the kingdom of Babylon. God blessed Daniel beyond measure and raised him up to a place of leadership and authority within the kingdom. Unfortunately, as so often happens, Daniel's success caused those around him to become envious of his position. These men began to look for a way to slander Daniel's reputation and to get rid of him for good. 1 Peter 2:12 Tells us to, **"Be careful to live properly among your unbelieving neighbors. Then even if they accuse you of doing wrong, they will see your honorable behavior, and they will give honor to God."** (NLT) The Holy Spirit who wrote that verse was the same Holy Spirit who spoke to Daniel and taught him how to be upright in the evil culture that he was forced to live in. Daniel 6 tells us that they could find nothing to accuse him of, unless it could be regarding the law of his God. These men, filled with selfish ambition and pride, ran to the king and said, **"Long live King Darius! We are all in agreement—we**

administrators, officials, high officers, advisers, and governors—that the king should make a law that will be strictly enforced. Give orders that for the next thirty days any person who prays to anyone, divine or human—except to you, Your Majesty—will be thrown into the den of lions. And now, Your Majesty, issue and sign this law so it cannot be changed, an official law of the Medes and Persians that cannot be revoked." 9 So King Darius signed the law." Daniel 6:6-9 (NLT)

Even though King Darius signed the law, Daniel couldn't fulfill this command because he had a lifelong habit of bowing down in prayer and thanksgiving to the True and Living God three times each day. I'll leave you to read the rest of Daniel 6 on your own to be reminded of how God sovereignly protected Daniel through the repercussions of not obeying man and choosing instead to please the higher authority of God. His story is absolutely inspiring and challenging, and it causes me to want to live for Jesus with all that I am!

Going back to that morning where my heart was immersed in Daniel 6, I kept thinking about his life in light of his habit of intentional prayer three times a day. Over and over again Daniel is described as one with an excellent spirit, as the one greatly beloved by God, as the one who had wisdom, insight, understanding, and as the one who had excellence more than all. Isn't that a description we would all love to have said about us? I wonder if Daniel gained these characteristics through his quiet time of prayer to God, three times a day, as customary habit. That morning God impressed strongly on my heart to make this type of prayer a diligent habit for thirty days.

Daniel was forbidden to pray for thirty days, which I know is not something that the majority of us reading this book are facing. Of course, we pray for our many brothers and sisters around the world who *are* facing such persecution and life-threatening consequences for serving God. But for many of us, praying multiple times a day isn't forbidden, but neither is it a driving priority in our lives. Jesus encouraged and challenged me that morning to intentionally start bowing down on my knees, three times a day, lifting up those needs that are dear to my heart and giving thanks for all of the glorious ways, wonders, and wills of God. God impressed upon my heart to write this book and to ask you if it's a habit that you would want to join me in? For 30 days, or for a lifetime, would you want to join me in praying over those family members, that friend's difficult marriage, or maybe your own, those prodigal children, or the petition against having prodigal children, those health problems, financial difficulties, that seemingly impossible-to-remove sin, those wayward family members, those friends cold to things of Jesus, and the countless other needs that come to our mind daily? Would we, three times a day, bend to our knees in order to battle on behalf of others through prayer?

But it wasn't just the prayer that made Daniel who he was. He spent time in prayer, but he also intentionally thanked God daily for all He had done. Could you imagine the beauty brought to our lives from taking three times a day to spend time magnifying the great things Jesus has done for us? Three times a day, creating space in our hearts and in our minds to recount the miracles of God that He has done and is still planning on doing in His perfect timing. Three times a day turning our hearts toward magnifying the character of God, toward His glorious attributes, and toward His love that He has shown to us so perfectly! Three times a day, whether on green shag carpet or a much nicer surface, spent looking up at our glorious God to make Him larger in our sight and perspective.

> **"Daniel made prayer and meditation of the Scriptures the chief business of his life; yet, if we consider the circumstances in which he was placed, we shall see that few ever had greater obstacles than he in the way of seeking God."**
> **Robert Cleaver Chapman**

My oldest daughter is a senior in high school as I write this, (cry cry). Her school requires her to take a life skills class and they learn, among many other things, how to be financially responsible. She came home one day telling me about a finance app that takes what you spend, rounds the change up to the nearest dollar and saves that money for you in an account. We decided to give it a try and after just a few months we had saved $100! It was amazing how such a small amount of money after each transaction could produce such great dividends.

I know we're busy, but just like the little bit of money we have left over, we really do have a few moments each day that we can dedicate to intentional, God-magnifying prayer. We can set timers on our phones, write a reminder on a chalkboard, or kneel at certain times each day, for two minutes, three minutes, or five minutes a day. It's just a couple minutes given over each day to stop the mouth of the enemy. It's just a couple minutes given over each day to magnify the character of God in our souls. It's just a couple minutes given over each day to pray non-believers into the Kingdom of God. It's just a couple minutes given over each day to clothe our brothers and sisters around the world in protective prayer. It's just a couple of minutes given over each day to lift our families before the throne of God. It's just a couple minutes a day, but with endless blessings attached.

I think this could be life changing.

I think this *was* life changing for Daniel.

> **"Light yourself on fire with passion and people will come from miles to watch you burn."**
> **John Wesley**

If we can choose to take a few minutes a day to get on our knees and pray, I think we'll see this habit produce greater dividends than we could ever imagine. And we don't have to do this alone- let's do this together! Grab people who want to commit intentionally to praying three times a day with you! Ask your family to do this with you. Ask your friends, or your church, or your kids to do this with you. Let's get on our knees together and change this world! Let's light ourselves up by magnifying the Lord through prayer and thanksgiving. An army of women who bow three times a day could be what this world needs to be set aflame for Jesus. I don't know about you, but I want to be part of a revival in my lifetime, and revival has always begun with intentional prayer!

King David said in Psalm 55:17 **"Evening and morning and at noon I will pray, and cry aloud, And He shall hear my voice."** I always wonder if Daniel could have taken his pattern of prayer from this verse. Obviously, we don't know now, but I hope we get to find out in heaven! This book is designed to be a guide to lift our hearts to magnify some of God's specific attributes three times a day, and to set us up with a pattern of thanksgiving. But I pray that this habit doesn't stop when this book ends! I'm praying that this book is just the beginning of what God wants to do in our lives and through our prayers as we press in to know Him more.

> **"My soul magnifies the Lord"**
> **Luke 1:46**

Day 1
Magnify!
Living Water

Have you ever been thirsty? And I mean insanely, over the top, can think about nothing else thirsty? When we first moved to our hot and sunny desert, I experienced one of the greatest moments of thirst that I ever remember having. Some of the sweet mommies from our new church invited us to hang out with them at a local water park. We went excited, but also a little apprehensive, since it was August and our unacclimated bodies still felt like we had moved to the surface of the sun! I'll never forget standing in the big wave pool, talking to some of my new friends, trying desperately to focus on what they were saying, but all I could think about was WATER! It was around 120 degrees that day, we were out in the sun, and I hadn't brought nearly enough water for us to drink. I was so thirsty that as we were standing in that water with a hundred other people, I actually caught myself instinctively bringing water up to my mouth to drink it! Thankfully some kind of Holy Spirit clarity stopped me just in time, but it was amazing to me how deep thirst could almost over ride my common sense in that moment.

> "On the last day, the climax of the festival, Jesus stood and shouted to the crowds, 'Anyone who is thirsty may come to me! Anyone who believes in me may come and drink! For the Scriptures declare, 'Rivers of living water will flow from his heart.'" (When he said 'living water,' he was speaking of the Spirit, who would be given to everyone believing in him....)"
> John 7:37-39 (NLT)

Humans were created thirsty. We were created with a void, not so that we would be empty, but so we would run to Jesus to be filled. We were created with a desire to search for fulfillment, and that fulfillment will only be found in walking daily with God. All around me that day in the water park were thermoses filled with clean, fresh, and pure ice water. In that moment of standing there so desperately thirsty, I didn't want to leave the conversations and take the time to walk to the clean water sources. Because of that I almost instead drank disgusting water with hundreds of people swimming in it! Sometimes seeking the Living Water found in Jesus can feel the same way. He sometimes seems inconvenient to seek, to search for, and to press into with all of our hearts. The deception of the enemy is to point out all we would have to forfeit if we were to go after that which would truly quench our thirst. He instead offers a substitute that doesn't seem ideal, but would surely do the trick for the moment. If we aren't daily at the watering hole of God, drinking in His Presence, being satisfied by His Spirit, letting His Word and voice satiate our longing, we will be willing to drink any less-than-ideal substitute that the enemy sends our way.

Over and over again in God's Word, He promises to take that which is parched, dry, cracked, and hopeless and flood it with the abundant living water of His Presence and goodness until those areas are teeming with life. He promises to bring beauty out of the ashes, joy from the mourning, life from the death. On that last day of the feast, Jesus stood and declared that ALL thirst could be quenched in Him. We are not left as orphans. We are not left alone. We are not forsaken. We have been left with the ever-present Helper, the Holy Spirit. He quenches our thirst. He satisfies. He helps us in those overwhelming moments of life. He takes all that was parched and damaged and He floods it with the life-giving blood of Jesus.

Numbers 21 is a tragic chapter of defeat, wars, complaining, and sin. And yet right in the middle of that section of Scripture, God commands Moses to gather up His people because He's going to give them water. They all gather and declare together, "Spring up O Well!" What a beautiful cry for provision that our hearts can declare with them today. Spring up O Well! In those places of dryness, spring up O Well of Living Water! In those places of sin, wars, battles, and defeat, spring up O Well of Living Water! In those places of fear, overwhelmed hearts, weariness and pain, spring up O Well of Living Water!

Jesus longs to truly flood us with His Presence, with His Spirit, with His Power, and His Preeminence. All that we could ever need, thirst for, long for, and desire, is found in being satiated in the Living Water that He offers freely to the thirsty who come to Him. He longs to gather us in the middle of our deserts and satisfy our thirsty souls. His Spirit comes not to those who are worthy, but always to those who are thirsty with need, thirsty with ache, and thirsty with desire for Him. Do you thirst today? Jesus is Who you seek.

Take a few minutes to praise God for the Living Water of His Presence and Spirit that He desires to quench our thirst with. Let Him examine your heart for any stagnant, infected water that the enemy might be trying to tempt you with, or that you have already been drinking deeply of. Have you taken time to guard your daily time of drinking deeply of Jesus? Lay this also before Jesus and let the Living Water of the Holy Spirit flood your heart and mind.

"Evening and morning and at noon I will pray, and cry aloud, and He shall hear my voice."
Psalm 55:17

Magnify!
Living Water

"A woman of Samaria came to draw water. Jesus said to her, "Give Me a drink." For His disciples had gone away into the city to buy food. Then the woman of Samaria said to Him, "How is it that You, being a Jew, ask a drink from me, a Samaritan woman?" For Jews have no dealings with Samaritans. Jesus answered and said to her, "If you knew the gift of God, and who it is who says to you, 'Give Me a drink,' you would have asked Him, and He would have given you living water." The woman said to Him, "Sir, You have nothing to draw with, and the well is deep. Where then do You get that living water? Are You greater than our father Jacob, who gave us the well, and drank from it himself, as well as his sons and his livestock?" Jesus answered and said to her, "Whoever drinks of this water will thirst again, but whoever drinks of the water that I shall give him will never thirst. But the water that I shall give him will become in him a fountain of water springing up into everlasting life." The woman said to Him, "Sir, give me this water, that I may not thirst, nor come here to draw."
John 4:7-15

"Then He who sat on the throne said, "Behold, I make all things new." And He said to me, "Write, for these words are true and faithful." And He said to me, "It is done! I am the Alpha and the Omega, the Beginning and the End. I will give of the fountain of the water of life freely to him who thirsts. He who overcomes shall inherit all things, and I will be his God and he shall be My son."
Revelation 21:5-7

"let us draw near with a true heart in full assurance of faith, having our hearts sprinkled from an evil conscience and our bodies washed with pure water."
Hebrews 10:22

"O God, You are my God; Early will I seek You;
My soul thirsts for You; My flesh longs for You
In a dry and thirsty land Where there is no water.
So I have looked for You in the sanctuary,
To see Your power and Your glory."
Psalm 63:1-2

"For I will pour water on him who is thirsty,
And floods on the dry ground;
I will pour My Spirit on your descendants, And My blessing on
your offspring; They will spring up among the grass like willows
by the watercourses.' One will say, 'I am the LORD's';
Another will call himself
by the name of Jacob; Another will write with his hand,
'The LORD's,' And name himself by the name of Israel."
Isaiah 44:3-5

"The LORD will guide you continually,
And satisfy your soul in drought,
And strengthen your bones;
You shall be like a watered garden,
And like a spring of water, whose waters do not fail."
Isaiah 58:11

"Jesus answered, "Most assuredly, I say to you, unless one is born of water and the Spirit, he cannot enter the kingdom of God. That which is born of the flesh is flesh, and that which is born of the Spirit is spirit. Do not marvel that I said to you, 'You must be born again.' The wind blows where it wishes, and you hear the sound of it, but cannot tell where it comes from and where it goes.
So is everyone who is born of the Spirit."
John 3:5-8

"The LORD is my shepherd;
I shall not want. He makes me to lie down in green pastures;
He leads me beside the still waters. He restores my soul;
He leads me in the paths of righteousness
For His name's sake."
Psalm 23:1-2

> "Enter into His gates with thanksgiving, and into His courts with praise. Be thankful to Him, and bless His name. For the LORD is good; His mercy is everlasting, and His truth endures to all generations."
> Psalm 100:4-5

Thank You Jesus today for…

_____
_____
_____
_____
_____
_____
_____
_____
_____
_____
_____
_____
_____
_____
_____
_____
_____
_____
_____
_____
_____
_____
_____
_____
_____
_____
_____
_____

Day 2
Magnify!
Beloved

If you had to choose one word to define who you are, what would it be? What would you like to be known as? What is it that you hope those in this world notice that you've accomplished by the end of your days, and what title would you like for them to give you? This world places a great emphasis upon our identity, and pressures us to do the same to others. People would like to categorize us according to our financial status, marital status, racial ethnicity, backgrounds, preferences, and occupations. Though the world will label us the way they wish, God labels us in the most beautiful way when He calls us His beloved. I just love this word *beloved*. I feel like it needs to be spoken with a sigh and a smile. You, precious daughter of God, are the beautiful *beloved* (sigh and smile) of the Father.

> "Let the beloved of the LORD rest secure in him, for he shields him all day long, and the one the LORD loves rests between his shoulders."
> Deuteronomy 33:12 (NIV)

The definition of *beloved* is: dearly loved; dear to the heart. It's an indication of the place that we have in God's heart. It's a promise of rest, peace, security, prominence, and protection within the love-filled hands of God. Beloved is not just *what* we are. It's *who* we are. It's a word that gives us a calling, a place, and an identity. It's a word that declares that we are known, accepted, desired, and longed for by the One who is so deeply in love with us. I used to love carrying my kids on my back when they were little. I loved the feel of them being so near, the sound of their voice, the smell of their breath, and the easy access to excited hugs when they were happy about something. What a glorious picture this verse gives us of God, our Father, carrying us upon His back. He loves to have us near, to hear our voice, and to draw us close as He blesses us with excitement over who He is.

The word beloved sheds light on the place of importance we have within the heart of God. The thought that we would have first place in anyone's heart is impressive, but the fact that we have prominence in God's heart is overwhelming! He's the Creator of all we know and see, and that which we can't even comprehend. He's the God of the universe, and we are the first love in His heart. What an astounding, heart splitting reality! When we fully immerse ourselves into this truth, our entire thought life, confidence, and perspective toward others should be altered forever. People cannot name us "less than." We have first place in the heart of God! You are His daughter, His love, His passion, and His delight. *Beloved* is an identity that should increase the stature of our thoughts and opinions. The title of beloved should give us confidence in who we are in Christ and boldness to let others know that they can find rest from the pressure and opinions of others when fully immersed into the love of Jesus.

The idea of the title *Beloved* also brings a separation and a distinction from those who have not chosen to submit themselves unto the God who desperately longs for them to live in light of this truth. God calls us away from the world's marking, away from the world's meandering, away from the world's maddening speech, and away from the world's message. In the Bible, *Beloved* is often used as a word of strength and remembrance of position that comes before a word of warning or instruction. Maybe it's God's way of saying, "I'm calling you to something higher!" It's a call to higher speech, higher thought, higher actions, and a higher way. The word Beloved reminds us that all we are called to is born out of the great love that He has for us, and the true identity He wants us to feel in Him.

The most beautiful concept of this word is that the One who calls us beloved is the true Beloved. He places His glory, His love, His beauty, and His radiance upon our faces and lives. It is Him who changes us, gives us His identity of clean, pure, holy, and righteous. He is the Beloved, and along with all He is, He gives us His identity of fully loved. We are our Beloved's, and He is ours! Do we declare that over our soul and mind every day? Regardless of what the world says and regardless of how we feel- WE ARE OUR BELOVED'S AND HE IS OURS! That's a life-changing, mind-altering, soul-warming truth that should shape who we are to the core of our beings. We are beloved. Not by Someone whose love is fickle, whose love grows cold, or whose thoughts are far from us. We are called beloved by the God who is the same yesterday, today, and forever. We are called beloved by the God who changes not. We are called beloved by the God who thinks about us more often than the number of sands in the seas. Precious friend, when you look in the mirror today and always, remember that you are beloved of God. The title of *Beloved* is a hidden crown that you wear on your face as you shine to the world the security of who you truly are in Christ. Whether you are in a circle of friends or seeming enemies, remember that you are beloved of God. When you lay down, rise up, sit down, or stand up, remember that you are the perfectly beloved of God. There is nothing that can change your position of beloved in God's mind. Let's walk and live as the beloved of God today, and carry that title, position, identity, placement, and calling with us everywhere we go.

"Evening and morning and at noon I will pray, and cry aloud, and He shall hear my voice."
Psalm 55:17

Magnify!
Beloved

"Put on then, as God's chosen ones, holy and beloved, compassionate hearts, kindness, humility, meekness, and patience."
Colossians 3:12 (ESV)

"Beloved, let us love one another, for love is from God, and whoever loves has been born of God and knows God. Anyone who does not love does not know God, because God is love."
1 John 4:7-8 (ESV)

"He was still speaking when, behold, a bright cloud overshadowed them, and a voice from the cloud said,
'This is my beloved son, with whom I am
well pleased; listen to him.'"
Matthew 17:5 (ESV)

"And he said to me, 'O Daniel, man greatly loved, understand the words that I speak to you, and stand upright, for now I have been sent to you.' And when he had spoken this word to me, I stood up trembling."
Daniel 10:11 (ESV)

"Therefore, my beloved brothers, be steadfast, immovable, always abounding in the work of the Lord, knowing that in the
Lord your labor is not in vain."
1 Corinthians 15:58 (ESV)

"Listen, my beloved brothers, has not God chosen those who are poor in the world to be rich in faith and heirs of the kingdom, which he has promised to those who love him?"
James 2:5 (ESV)

"I am my beloved's, and my beloved is mine"
Song of Solomon 6:3

"To the praise of his glorious grace, with which he has blessed us in the beloved."
Ephesians 1:6 (ESV)

"Behold, you are beautiful, my beloved, truly delightful."
Song of Solomon 1:15 (ESV)

"Paul, a prisoner for Christ Jesus, and Timothy our brother, to Philemon our beloved fellow worker."
Philemon 1:1 (ESV)

"Therefore, my beloved, as you have always obeyed, so now, not only as in my presence, but much more in my absence, work out your own salvation with fear and trembling."
Philippians 2:12 (ESV)

"But you, beloved, building yourselves up in your most holy faith and praying in the Holy Spirit"
Jude 1:20 (ESV)

"Beloved, I urge you as sojourners and exiles to abstain from the passions of the flesh, which wage war against your soul."
1 Peter 2:11 (ESV)

"As indeed he says in Hosea, 'Those who were not my people, I will call 'my people,' and her who was not beloved I will call 'beloved.'"
Romans 9:25 (ESV)

"Therefore, my brothers, whom I love and long for, my joy and crown, stand firm thus in the Lord, my beloved."
Philippians 4:1 (ESV)

"That Your beloved may be delivered,
Save with Your right hand, and hear me."
Psalm 60:5

> "Enter into His gates with thanksgiving, and into His courts with praise. Be thankful to Him, and bless His name. For the LORD is good; His mercy is everlasting, and His truth endures to all generations."
> Psalm 100:4-5

Thank You Jesus today for…

Day 3
Magnify!
Grace

How do you adequately write about, meditate upon, or praise God for the very substance that God's Word speaks of as enabling us to stand before the righteous Holy God without spot or blemish? In the days when animal sacrifice was required and had to be bought, brought, and slaughtered to atone for our sin, maybe what grace truly cost was a little better understood. I am ever-thankful that Jesus is the Perfect, spotless Lamb and the Once-for-all atoning sacrifice for me. While I'm grateful for not needing to haul a sacrificial lamb down to a temple and watch the life drain out of it because of something that I have done, I feel the absence of it can also cause us to unintentionally forget the costliness of all that we've received. James 4:9 tells us to lament, mourn, weep, and even wail over our sin. True grace is magnified in our sights when we take a long look at who we have been and all that we have done; not for condemnation, but for a greater appreciation of all that we have been forgiven, and an excitement of how new God has made us!

> "And I will pour out on the house of David and the inhabitants of Jerusalem a spirit of grace and pleas for mercy, so that, when they look on me, on him whom they have pierced, they shall mourn for him, as one mourns for an only child, and weep bitterly over him, as one weeps over a firstborn."
> Zechariah 12:10 (ESV)

God tells Zechariah that the grace and mercy He was going to pour out would bring weeping for a moment over how great the cost was upon the Messiah. True grace doesn't bring a desired continuance in sin, but rather cleansing tears over all we have been forgiven. True grace brings a desire for more of Jesus, an awe of all He has done, a mourning of sin, and a thankfulness for all we've been given. Grace gives us new eyes to look at life with, to look at God with, and to look at each other with! The reality of grace is newness! Magnified grace is new sight, new perspective, new identity, new hope, and new love. Grace brings a forgiven past, a changed present, and a new future. Amazing grace! How sweet is the sound of our sins falling away! Our chains are gone, our bondage is over, and our stains are done away with. Zechariah 12 gives us the reality that grace begins in mourning. It begins in mourning over the severity of sin and our tendency toward disobedience and flippancy toward the serious things of God. When we truly enter into the thoughts of who we've been, and who we would continue to be without Jesus, grace deepens because the reality of what grace has cost and who grace has actually made us becomes clearer to our hearts.

True Grace also gives us God's eyes as we look at those who are still struggling in the depths of sin. Grace gives us a heart of love to save and rescue rather than to disgrace (ungrace, to remove grace, to separate grace from that person.) Rather than disgrace, true grace gives us a desire to impart grace to the hearers by speaking God's words that will restore and make whole again. Jesus had such beautiful eyes of grace as He walked this world! From the woman caught in adultery, to the thief on the cross, His eyes didn't condemn those looking for grace, they restored. His eyes didn't separate those longing for grace, they gave unity.

Zechariah 13:1 says, "On that day there shall be a fountain opened for the house of David and the inhabitants of Jerusalem, to cleanse them from sin and uncleanness." When grace is poured out there is always a place of cleansing available. With Jesus there is always the ability to remove what we've done, to renew who we've been, and for Him to remake us into who He longs for us to be once again by His grace. This glorious grace that is greater than all our sin! There is nothing- pause and think about that for a second- NOTHING that we could do that would take us beyond the grip of grace. There is NOTHING that can take us beyond the ability of God to wash us, cleanse us, restore us. NOTHING that disables Him from making us new, making us holy, and making us usable once again. There are no human words to adequately describe this astounding reality of grace that we live in. You and I, from the greatest depravity to the smallest depravity are still filled with the depravity of sin, and yet God sends forth His grace like a mighty flood of the strongest soap that we could ever imagine, and God scrubs our souls clean. He gently and lovingly scrubs our memories, our mistakes, our mountains of wrongs, and our mighty sin nature. And He scrubs them until they shine and gleam with His glory. This is the beauty of God-given grace!

Right now, the window that I'm kneeling daily in front of has a view of beautiful snow-capped mountains. The appearance has changed entirely because of this gleaming white snow dumped on the top. Grace works in that way, but even better. Grace doesn't just cover the mud, murk, dirt, and debris with its gleaming glory. It removes it entirely! Our appearance has changed, but even more than that, WE have been changed! Who we are has changed. Who we can be has changed! Who we are called to be from this point on has changed! Grace takes the wretched and instead cries out, "New, Redeemed, and Beloved!"

"Evening and morning and at noon I will pray, and cry aloud, and He shall hear my voice."
Psalm 55:17

Magnify!
Grace

"The Word became flesh and made his dwelling among us. We have seen his glory, the glory of the one and only Son, who came from the Father, full of grace and truth."
John 1:14 (NIV)

"Concerning this thing I pleaded with the Lord three times that it might depart from me. And He said to me, 'My grace is sufficient for you, for My strength is made perfect in weakness.' Therefore most gladly I will rather boast in my infirmities,
that the power of Christ may rest upon me."
2 Corinthians 12:8-9

"This is the word of the LORD to Zerubbabel: 'Not by might nor by power, but by My Spirit' says the LORD of hosts. Who are you, O great mountain? Before Zerubbabel you shall become a plain! And he shall bring forth the capstone With shouts of "Grace, grace to it!"'"
Zechariah 4:6-7

"that in the ages to come He might show the exceeding riches of His grace in His kindness toward us in Christ Jesus. For by grace you have been saved through faith, and that not of yourselves; it is the gift of God, not of works, lest anyone should boast."
Ephesians 2:7-9

"For we do not have a High Priest who cannot sympathize with our weaknesses, but was in all points tempted as we are, yet without sin. Let us therefore come boldly to the throne of grace, that we may obtain mercy and find grace to help in time of need."
Hebrews 4:15-16

"But now the righteousness of God apart from the law is revealed, being witnessed by the Law and the Prophets, even the righteousness of God, through faith in Jesus Christ, to all and on all who believe. For there is no difference; for all have sinned and fall short of the glory of God, being justified freely by His grace through the redemption that is in Christ Jesus, whom God set forth as a propitiation by His blood, through faith, to demonstrate His righteousness, because in His forbearance God had passed over the sins that were previously committed, to demonstrate at the present time His righteousness, that He might be just and the justifier of the one who has faith in Jesus."
Romans 3:21-26

"And the LORD was sorry that He had made man on the earth, and He was grieved in His heart. So the LORD said, "I will destroy man whom I have created from the face of the earth, both man and beast, creeping thing and birds of the air, for I am sorry that I have made them." But Noah found grace in the eyes of the LORD. This is the genealogy of Noah. Noah was a just man, perfect in his generations. Noah walked with God."
Genesis 6:6-9

"For the grace of God that brings salvation has appeared to all men, teaching us that, denying ungodliness and worldly lusts, we should live soberly, righteously, and godly in the present age, looking for the blessed hope and glorious appearing of our great God and Savior Jesus Christ, who gave Himself for us, that He might redeem us from every lawless deed and purify for Himself His own special people, zealous for good works."
Titus 2:11-14

"Therefore do not let sin reign in your mortal body, that you should obey it in its lusts. And do not present your members as instruments of unrighteousness to sin, but present yourselves to God as being alive from the dead, and your members as instruments of righteousness to God. For sin shall not have dominion over you, for you are not under law but under grace."
Romans 6:12-14

> "Enter into His gates with thanksgiving, and into His courts with praise. Be thankful to Him, and bless His name.
> For the LORD is good; His mercy is everlasting, and His truth endures to all generations."
> Psalm 100:4-5

Thank You Jesus today for…

_____
_____
_____
_____
_____
_____
_____
_____
_____
_____
_____
_____
_____
_____
_____
_____
_____
_____
_____
_____
_____
_____
_____
_____
_____
_____
_____

Day 4
Magnify!
Joy

What makes you truly over the top happy? Maybe vacations? Family time? Shopping? Spa days? Theme parks? Hanging out with friends? Feeling healthy? As you know, the problem with the things that make us happy in this world is that they all eventually come to an end! Most of this life's happiness is circumstantial. Why do we say things like, "Oh I wish it could always be this way!"? Because we know that eventually things will change. Every happy moment in this world has a speck of angst within it because our hearts know that life will just keep marching on! Lasting joy is found in the True Joy Giver alone.

> "You will show me the path of life; In Your presence is fullness of joy; At Your right hand are pleasures forevermore."
> Psalm 16:11

While happiness is found in the perfect circumstances, true joy is found in being in the Presence of the Perfect One. Life's good times slowly drift away, but the glorious Presence of God is available to us in a deeper way at every waking moment. Each day the avenues of prayer, praise, and God's Word are open for us, enabling us to run to into His Presence. No longer are we captives pursuing the temporary happiness of this life and bound up in the passing pleasures of this world alone. The fullness of God's lasting joy found in His ever-present Presence is ours for the asking, every second of the day!

Joy isn't positive thinking, but it *is* a choice to think ourselves right into His presence. Do you remember when Peter walked on water with Jesus in the Gospels, and began to sink as he focused on the wind and the waves? So too we will sink as we look at the storms of this life and dwell on its many waves, wobbles, floods, and frowns. But if we will just choose instead to lift our gaze above life's storms and lift our eyes right into the pure Presence of God, what joy would flood our hearts! Eyes up precious one! Eyes off of this world and onto His glorious face! Eyes off of this world and up instead to the King of Glory who bends His ears to hear our prayers. Eyes up onto the One who moved heaven and earth to obtain our souls. Eyes up onto your heavenly destiny and upon the glorious God who loves you so much!

I know this life is often wrought with problems, chaos, hard times, and difficulties. I know that sometimes we feel pain, despair, loneliness, and fear. But in those moments would we remember that true joy comes when we intentionally acknowledge that this life is but a breath. In this world we will face tribulations- that was a promise from Jesus. But good cheer comes from remembering that Jesus has gone to prepare a place for us where we will be with Him for all of eternity. Joy doesn't come when we cling to this temporary life with a fervent desire to make it permanent. God's true joy, available to us at all times, comes when we choose instead to lift our eyes up to our permanent heavenly home. A reward is promised to us. A guaranteed inheritance awaits us. And this hope of a home where every tear is wiped away and the glory of God lights our day is the sure fulfillment for every child of God who has called upon His name for salvation.

Remembering that the Presence of God is available to us in this life and that the Presence of God in its fullness awaits us in the next is what causes us to remain joyful in this life. I remember a time, in second grade, when I was wringing my hands over a spelling test where I would have to differentiate between the words here and hear. Wouldn't it be nice if we were only anxious over such menial things now? But if we really think about it, someday the things we're so anxious over right now will be just that- menial. Aside from the fact that most of the things we worry about will never come to pass, the reality is that even what we do actually experience will seem insignificant in the future as we look back. I'm not trying to make the things that concern us today sound trite. I know that often times we're facing serious things in life that can cause much fear, angst, anxiety, and worry. But in those times, joy comes by choosing to dwell on the truth that we serve an awesome, powerful, and mighty God who promises to work all things together for good to those who love Him and are called according to His purposes. While there is worry in this life, there is also joy found in taking this good God at His Word and choosing to praise in the fullness of His Presence where joy is found.

So today, would we fix our eyes on those things above where God is? Would we find joy in the midst of pain, fear, worry, and sorrow by choosing to enter into the glory of God's Presence where the fullness of joy and pleasure are found? Maybe take some extra time today to list even more things that you're grateful for. Or maybe find joy by singing a song of praise to the One who has been so good and has promised to be nothing but faithful to you in the future. You are not meant to dwell here forever. You are a sojourner on a journey to your permanent home where glory awaits. So, eyes up today precious one, and may joy be found in your hearts as you press into His Presence with every choice you make!

"Evening and morning and at noon I will pray, and cry aloud, and He shall hear my voice."
Psalm 55:17

Magnify!
Joy

"Rejoice in the Lord always. I will say it again: Rejoice!"
Philippians 4:4 (NIV)

"For the LORD your God is living among you. He is a mighty Savior. He will take delight in you with gladness. With his love, he will calm all your fears. He will rejoice over you with joyful songs."
Zephaniah 3:17 (NLT)

"Be joyful in hope, patient in affliction, faithful in prayer."
Romans 12:12 (NIV)

"When anxiety was great within me,
your consolation brought me joy."
Psalm 94:19 (NIV)

"Though the fig tree does not bud and there are no grapes on the vines, though the olive crop fails and the fields produce no food, though there are no sheep in the pen and no cattle in the stalls, yet I will rejoice in the Lord, I will be joyful in God my Savior."
Habakkuk 3:17-18 (NIV)

"Though you have not seen him, you love him; and even though you do not see him now, you believe in him and are filled with an inexpressible and glorious joy for you are receiving the end result of your faith, the salvation of your souls."
1 Peter 1:8-9 (NIV)

"This is a sacred day before our Lord. Don't be dejected and sad, for the joy of the LORD is your strength!"
Nehemiah 8:10 (NLT)

"I am overwhelmed with joy in the LORD my God! For he has dressed me with the clothing of salvation and draped me in a robe of righteousness. I am like a bridegroom dressed for his wedding or a bride with her jewels."
Isaiah 61:10 (NLT)

"Until now you have asked nothing in my name. Ask, and you will receive, that your joy may be full."
John 16:24 (ESV)

"I rejoice in following your statutes
as one rejoices in great riches."
Psalm 119:14 (NIV)

"A man has joy by the answer of his mouth,
And a word spoken in due season, how good it is!"
Proverbs 15:23

"But the fruit of the Spirit is love, joy, peace, forbearance, kindness, goodness, faithfulness, gentleness and self-control. Against such things there is no law."
Galatians 5:22-23 (NIV)

"Deceit is in the hearts of those who plot evil,
but those who promote peace have joy."
Proverbs 12:20 (NIV)

"so that I may come to you with joy, by God's will, and in your company be refreshed. The God of peace be with you all. Amen."
Romans 15:32-33 (NIV)

"Your testimonies are my heritage forever,
for they are the joy of my heart."
Psalm 119:111 (ESV)

"If you keep my commands, you will remain in my love, just as I have kept my Father's commands and remain in his love. I have told you this so that my joy may be in you and that your joy may be complete."
John 15:10-11 (ESV)

"A joyful heart is good medicine,
but a crushed spirit dries up the bones."
Proverbs 17:22 (ESV)

"Enter into His gates with thanksgiving, and into His courts with praise. Be thankful to Him, and bless His name. For the LORD is good; His mercy is everlasting, and His truth endures to all generations."
Psalm 100:4-5

Thank You Jesus today for…

_____
_____
_____
_____
_____
_____
_____
_____
_____
_____
_____
_____
_____
_____
_____
_____
_____
_____
_____
_____
_____
_____
_____
_____
_____
_____
_____
_____
_____

Day 5
Magnify!
God's Faithfulness

Have you ever felt the glorious relief of moving into the shade after being in the scorching sun for a prolonged period of time? I remember one moment in particular, I was waiting outside for my oldest daughter to finish a walk-a-thon for her school in our hot desert. I had planned on staying right near the finish line so that I could be the first, smiling face that saw when she crossed over, (trying to earn good mommy points!) but it was taking so much longer than I thought it would. The finish line was in the sun, on top of the dirt, and colored chalk was bursting into the air with every kid who crossed that line. As my lungs were filling up with more and more colored chalk dust, I couldn't believe how hot, dry, parched, and sweaty I felt. I saw a place on the shady grass where I could still have a good view of the finish line and decided to move there instead. I couldn't believe the difference! Instantly my body cooled down, and the feeling of the scorching sun and stifling chalk dust melted away in the coolness. I often picture God's faithfulness being like that feeling of moving from the sun-scorched, parched land to the shady grass. Maybe you have moments like I do, when you're filled with fear, doubt, anxiety, worry, pain, or wonder. What a feeling of relief it is when God's faithful Presence comes in like a flood to remind us that He is in control, that He will remain faithful, and that He is working all things together for good.

> "And the LORD went before them by day in a pillar of cloud to lead them along the way, and by night in a pillar of fire to give them light, that they might travel by day and by night. The pillar of cloud by day and the pillar of fire by night did not depart from before the people."
> Exodus 13:21-22 (ESV)

The beautiful, steadying power of the presence of God absolutely astounds me. In God's faithfulness, He gave them exactly what they needed, in the exact way they needed it. When His people would feel the heat of the day from traveling through the scorching, dry wilderness, God's faithful Presence was there to give them relief from the sun and to envelope them into the shade that they would desperately be longing for. When God's people were wandering through the night, or setting up camp in the pitch-black darkness, God's faithful Presence was there to light up the night and bring warmth to their skin. What a glorious testimony of this faithful God we serve!

Sometimes the actual reality of God's faithfulness gets muddled with our own expectations of what rescue will look like. God will always be faithful, but His faithfulness might not always work out in the exact way we think it will, or even think it should. God's ways are higher, His plans are deeper than we could ever imagine, and are often different than the plans we have for ourselves. I'm sure the children of Israel would rather have instantly and magically appeared in the land flowing with milk and honey, rather than needing God be their Shade, Warmth, Light, and Protection. Many times, God allows us to wander in the places where we need to see His faithfulness. His faithfulness can look different than we thought it would, but His goodness will always be proclaimed by us in the end! God's ways are far better than our own plans, whether we realize it in the moment or not.

The book of Romans tells us that faith comes by hearing the Word of God. Precious friend, are we immersed in God's Word? Are we reading every day the stories of His faithfulness, of His provision, of His care, and His character? We are strengthened by knowing that God will always be faithful in our lives, and that strength comes when we choose to call to remembrance His faithfulness in the lives of others. Remembering God's past character of faithfulness in our own lives, and reading the true, Biblical stories of how He's been faithful to others will cause us to be full of faith that He will come through for us in the future! We meditate on His faithfulness by reading truths where, time and time again, He proved Himself to be faithful to His people. God is faithful, and will be faithful, which means that we can daily be full of faith that we will see His faithfulness once again! Even when we are faithless, (have less faith) He will remain faithful, (full of faithfulness) because He cannot deny Himself! His very character is faithfulness. There is no way for Him to not be faithful. It's who He is in the fiber of His being. Have no fear, Your God is on the way to be exactly who you need Him to be in the exact moment you need Him to come through. He's greater than any super hero, and more steady and secure than anything in this life that we could ever depend upon. It is faith in this faithful God that moves mountains and settles souls. It is faith in this faithful God that steadies our hearts and causes us not to be tossed to and fro with worry, doubt, fear, and anxiety. It is faith in this faithful God that causes us to know that He is listening when we pray, though we can't hear Him audibly or see Him physically. What life sized mountain is it that you need to see moved today? What great need do you have that you long to see God provide for? How is it that you need to see our God be the faithful Rescuer and Savior that He declares He is? Take heart. God is coming in His faithfulness and you will not have lack for long.

"Evening and morning and at noon I will pray, and cry aloud, and He shall hear my voice."
Psalm 55:17

Magnify!
God's Faithfulness

"Understand, therefore, that the LORD your God is indeed God. He is the faithful God who keeps his covenant for a thousand generations and lavishes his unfailing love on those who
love him and obey his commands."
Deuteronomy 7:9 (NLT)

"If we are unfaithful, he remains faithful,
for he cannot deny who he is."
2 Timothy 2:13 (NLT)

"For the word of the LORD is right and true;
he is faithful in all he does."
Psalm 33:4 (NIV)

"He will cover you with his feathers,
and under his wings you will find refuge;
his faithfulness will be your shield and rampart."
Psalm 91:4 (NIV)

"But the Lord is faithful. He will establish you
and guard you against the evil one."
2 Thessalonians 3:3 (ESV)

"If we confess our sins, He is faithful and just to forgive us our sins
and to cleanse us from all unrighteousness."
1 John 1:9

"The temptations in your life are no different from what others experience. And God is faithful. He will not allow the temptation to be more than you can stand. When you are tempted,
he will show you a way out so that you can endure."
1 Corinthians 10:13 (NLT)

"Your faithfulness extends to every generation,
as enduring as the earth you created."
Psalms 119:90 (NLT)

"God is faithful, by whom you were called into the fellowship
of His Son, Jesus Christ our Lord."
1 Corinthians 1:9

"Let us hold fast the confession of our hope without wavering,
for He who promised is faithful."
Hebrews 10:23

"Through the LORD's mercies we are not consumed, Because His
compassions fail not. They are new every morning;
Great is Your faithfulness."
Lamentations 3:22-23

"Therefore let those who suffer according to God's will
entrust their souls to a faithful Creator while doing good."
1 Peter 4:19 (ESV)

"Your unfailing love, O LORD, is as vast as the heavens;
your faithfulness reaches beyond the clouds."
Psalm 36:5 (NLT)

"May God himself, the God of peace, sanctify you through and
through. May your whole spirit, soul and body be kept blameless at the
coming of our Lord Jesus Christ. The one who calls you
is faithful, and he will do it."
1 Thessalonians 5:23-24 (NIV)

"O LORD God of hosts, Who is mighty like You, O LORD?
Your faithfulness also surrounds You."
Psalm 89:8

"Then the LORD came down in the cloud and stood there with him
and proclaimed his name, the LORD. And he passed in front of Moses,
proclaiming, 'The LORD, the LORD, the compassionate and gracious
God, slow to anger, abounding in love and faithfulness, maintaining love
to thousands, and forgiving wickedness, rebellion and sin.'"
Exodus 34:5-7 (NIV)

"Enter into His gates with thanksgiving, and into His courts with praise. Be thankful to Him, and bless His name. For the LORD is good; His mercy is everlasting, and His truth endures to all generations."
Psalm 100:4-5

Thank You Jesus today for…

_____
_____
_____
_____
_____
_____
_____
_____
_____
_____
_____
_____
_____
_____
_____
_____
_____
_____
_____
_____
_____
_____
_____
_____
_____
_____
_____
_____
_____

Day 6
Magnify!
His Compassion

Do you ever look at this hurting, pain-filled world and wonder what you can do to help? I'm often overwhelmed when I hear of those in horrific situations, and yet have no way to reach them. My heart is burdened by all those who are trapped by fear, anxiety, and worry. My heart grieves for those who are sick, in pain, isolated, displaced, or trapped in prisons of their own choosing. But at other times I'm shocked at the hardness of my own heart, my apathy, my lack of care for others, and my tendency toward self-preservation. I long to have the heart of Jesus, who was moved with compassion toward His creation.

> "Now Jesus called His disciples to Himself and said, 'I have compassion on the multitude, because they have now continued with Me three days and have nothing to eat. And I do not want to send them away hungry, lest they faint on the way.' Then His disciples said to Him, 'Where could we get enough bread in the wilderness to fill such a great multitude?' Jesus said to them, 'How many loaves do you have?' And they said, 'Seven, and a few little fish.' So He commanded the multitude to sit down on the ground. And He took the seven loaves and the fish and gave thanks, broke them and gave them to His disciples; and the disciples gave to the multitude. So they all ate and were filled, and they took up seven large baskets full of the fragments that were left."
> Matthew 15:32-38

"Who is going to help these people... this situation... this time?" Those are questions I often hear, and I think the answer should be- US! Jesus was moved with a compassion that moved Him to action. His compassion stopped Him in His tracks and caused Him to see others in their plight rather than being content with His own well-being. His is a compassion that caused Him to sacrifice His own time, resources, energy, and eventually His life on behalf of others. Jesus allowed His compassion to not just move Him emotionally to desire, sympathy, and tears, but to move Him to give of Himself. When we have compassion toward another, we are sharing in just a moment of what the eyes and heart of God feel constantly. It's the eyes of Jesus that know all, see all, feel all, and hear all that move with such action on our behalf. These people were hungry, and the heart of Jesus was moved at their desire to follow Him in spite of their own personal needs.

I love that Jesus draws the attention of His disciples to the needs of the people with not a command but a statement, not an order but a wonder; and the responsive thoughts of the disciples were much like our own thoughts today. We're moved so often not by God's compassion, but by our own needs, desires, and practical thoughts. We don't have enough, we're kind of tired ourselves, and we'd also love to sit down and have a meal. But Jesus draws them out beyond themselves, where He dwells; beyond His own comfort, beyond His own desires, beyond His own needs. He brings them into a miraculous realm of the 'It's better to give than to receive' world. God will always provide what is needed when we choose to give, dwell, live, and notice beyond our own needs. He draws their eyes to the need, only to draw their eyes to the solution of how He planned on providing for His people. This is the beautiful thing about God's heart of compassion! The solution isn't up to us. He doesn't draw out our compassion to incite panic or pity. He draws out our compassion because He wants to use us to solve the problem that He already sees and already has a plan for! God's heart is forever moved with compassion and He wants us to be the vessels that are willing to make known His heart of love and His hands that bring provision.

It was this same heart for us, the sheep without a Shepherd, that would drive Jesus to the cross. He's always been moved with compassion for us. He's moved with compassion toward our prayers, our tears, our needs, our wants, our desires, our lack, and our burdened hearts. His compassion caused Him to cry out to the thirsty to come to Him, to cry out to the hungry to partake of Him, to cry out to the lost to find shelter in Him, to cry out to the isolated to come near Him. This whole story of redemption has been unfolding for ages by the God who has been moved with compassion long before the first day of creation. This was not a second thought, New Testament plan to redeem the lost. He's the same God yesterday, today, and forever. Compassion has always been the driving force of every action and moment before the foundation of the earth.

The compassionate ear of God is bent to hear you now! What is it that you need today? What are you lacking? What is the cry of your heart? He longs to move with compassion toward you, and He longs to move you with His compassion toward others. Take a few minutes right now to praise the God whose compassionate heart ever lives to draw you close to Him and provide for your every need eternally.

"Evening and morning and at noon I will pray, and cry aloud, and He shall hear my voice."
Psalm 55:17

Magnify!
His Compassion

"Then Jesus went about all the cities and villages, teaching in their synagogues, preaching the gospel of the kingdom, and healing every sickness and every disease among the people. But when He saw the multitudes, He was moved with compassion for them,
because they were weary and scattered,
like sheep having no shepherd."
Matthew 9:35-37

"But you, Lord, are a compassionate and gracious God, slow to anger, abounding in love and faithfulness."
Psalm 86:15 (NIV)

"Yet this I call to mind and therefore I have hope: Because of the LORD's great love we are not consumed, for his compassions never fail. They are new every morning; great is your faithfulness. I say to myself, 'The LORD is my portion;
therefore I will wait for him.'"
Lamentations 3:21-24 (NIV)

"But He, being full of compassion, forgave their iniquity, And did not destroy them. Yes, many a time He turned His anger away, And did not stir up all His wrath; For He remembered that they were but flesh, A breath that passes away and does not come again."
Psalm 78:38-39

"Shout for joy, you heavens; rejoice, you earth; burst into song, you mountains! For the LORD comforts his people
and will have compassion on his afflicted ones."
Isaiah 49:13 (NIV)

"As a father has compassion on his children, so the LORD has compassion on those who fear him"
Psalm 103:13 (NIV)

"And he arose and came to his father. But when he was still a great way off, his father saw him and had compassion, and ran and fell on his neck and kissed him. And the son said to him, 'Father, I have sinned against heaven and in your sight, and am no longer worthy to be called your son.' But the father said to his servants, 'Bring out the best robe and put it on him, and put a ring on his hand and sandals on his feet. And bring the fatted calf here and kill it, and let us eat and be merry; for this my son was dead and is alive again; he was lost and is found.'
And they began to be merry."
Luke 15:20-24

"So the LORD said to Moses, 'I will also do this thing that you have spoken; for you have found grace in My sight, and I know you by name.' And he said, 'Please, show me Your glory.' Then He said, "I will make all My goodness pass before you, and I will proclaim the name of the LORD before you. I will be gracious to whom I will be gracious, and I will have compassion on whom I will have compassion."
Exodus 33:17-19

"Praise be to the God and Father of our Lord Jesus Christ, the Father of compassion and the God of all comfort, who comforts us in all our troubles, so that we can comfort those in any trouble with the comfort we ourselves receive from God. For just as we share abundantly in the sufferings of Christ, so also our comfort abounds through Christ."
2 Corinthians 1.3-5 (NIV)

"So the LORD must wait for you to come to him
so he can show you his love and compassion.
For the LORD is a faithful God.
Blessed are those who wait for his help."
Isaiah 30:18 (NLT)

"Rend your heart and not your garments. Return to the LORD your God, for he is gracious and compassionate, slow to anger and abounding in love, and he relents from sending calamity."
Joel 2:13 (NIV)

"You have heard of the perseverance of Job and seen the end intended by the Lord—that the Lord is very compassionate and merciful."
James 5:11

"Enter into His gates with thanksgiving, and into His courts with praise. Be thankful to Him, and bless His name. For the LORD is good; His mercy is everlasting, and His truth endures to all generations."
Psalm 100:4-5

Thank You Jesus today for...

_____
_____
_____
_____
_____
_____
_____
_____
_____
_____
_____
_____
_____
_____
_____
_____
_____
_____
_____
_____
_____
_____
_____
_____
_____
_____
_____
_____
_____

Day 7
Magnify!
Trust in God

Have you ever done exactly what you felt like God told you to do and still had things seem to turn out terribly wrong? I remember a couple of times God put on my heart to fast for different people and different situations. Now, I love food, so I don't run into a time of fasting easily, but I chose to obey, and I sat back with my hungry tummy and waited for God's mighty hand of awesomeness to move within these people. As I fasted and prayed, fasted and prayed, and fasted and prayed some THINGS GOT WORSE! One of the people left our church, and the other situation got really ugly before God seemed to bring beauty out of it, which was WAY after my fast was over. I'm sure you won't want to ask me to fast for you any time soon! Sometimes not getting the results we were looking for detours us from wanting to follow God's ways. In our short-sightedness we usually want things to add up to our 'perfect' understanding of the matter, but one plus one does not always equal two in God's economy. The Word of God is filled with verses declaring God's ways to be higher than ours, His wisdom to be beyond ours, and His understanding to be far beyond our ability to figure it out. Basic trust in God boils down to the ability to reconcile what we know to be true of God with what we see living out circumstantially before our eyes. Trust is a choice to see beyond our earthly vision and instead choose to believe with faith-filled hearts that God will absolutely do something to work all things together for good, whether we can see it or not. I think Habakkuk 3 in the Amplified version declares this so beautifully.

"Though the fig tree does not blossom and there is no fruit on the vines, Though the yield of the olive fails and the fields produce no food, Though the flock is cut off from the fold and there are no cattle in the stalls, Yet I will [choose to] rejoice in the LORD;
I will [choose to] shout in exultation in the [victorious] God of my salvation! The Lord GOD is my strength [my source of courage, my invincible army]; He has made my feet [steady and sure] like hinds' feet And makes me walk [forward with spiritual confidence] on my high places [of challenge and responsibility]."
Habakkuk 3:17-19 (AMP)

In his book, Habakkuk struggles to see the alignment of God's goodness in the details of His plan. Struggle is normal, but like Habakkuk, it's paramount that we land on the safe, solid, and joyful truth that God is God, and we are not. The firm belief that God's ways are so much higher than anything that our finite minds can understand is essential to the success of our Christianity. Habakkuk struggles, but lands right. Like him we must remind ourselves and declare to our souls that if something doesn't seem to align right within what we see and what we know, that God will still be faithful, and we will still be okay. Trust is a having a bigger view of God's ability, understanding, and ways, and a smaller view of our own. Trust is saying, like Peter in Luke 5:5- We've already tried this, and it didn't work, "but nevertheless, at Your Word…" What an essential sentence to end our statements of confusion with. We might be completely bewildered and overwhelmed, "but nevertheless, at Your Word…" We might be devastated and heartbroken, "but nevertheless, at Your Word…" Isn't this where Jesus landed in His own heart in the Garden of Gethsemane when He said, "Not My will but Yours be done"? Trusting God is a sure and steady soul choice to emphatically declare, regardless of feelings, "Your will be done in all things." When we can't understand… "Your will be done." When we can't see the light in the darkness… "Your will be done." When we see life's injustices and feel its unfairness… "Your will be done."

I want to grow in this, don't you? Maybe growing in trust is simply learning not to even state our opinions, our protests, our buts, our complaints, or our advice. Maybe growing in trust is learning to leave off the reasonings, the accusations, the doubts, and statements of all of the ways we would have done things differently. Maybe maturity is learning to let the first response be, "At Your Word" as opposed to listing all of our different opinions and ending with, "*Nevertheless* at Your Word." If we can get to that initial soul response of trust in the good, sovereign, and mighty God, I think we'll be blown away at His perfect artistry in weaving His tapestry of goodness within our lives. We too like Peter will end up falling on our knees in awe over what Jesus is able to do.

We serve a trustworthy God. Our trust is not a blind trust that is commanded in spite of reasonable belief. God has never failed us. His Word promises that He never will. For generation after generation God has proved Himself good and trustworthy, and it's this God who asks us to lean upon His understanding rather than our own. Is there something that needs to be surrendered in trust today? Is there something that needs to be rejoiced over in faith, despite what you see with your eyes. We'll never regret a decision to surrender our impaired sight and trust ourselves to the only wise God, who promises in His sovereignty, to work His goodness into every detail of our lives.

> *"Evening and morning and at noon I will pray, and cry aloud,
> and He shall hear my voice."*
> Psalm 55:17

Magnify!
Trust in God

> "Trust in the LORD with all your heart, and lean not on your own understanding; In all your ways acknowledge Him,
> And He shall direct your paths."
> Proverbs 3:5-6

> "That is why I tell you not to worry about everyday life—whether you have enough food and drink, or enough clothes to wear. Isn't life more than food, and your body more than clothing? Look at the birds. They don't plant or harvest or store food in barns, for your heavenly Father feeds them. And aren't you far more valuable to him than they are? Can all your worries add a single moment to your life? And why worry about your clothing? Look at the lilies of the field and how they grow. They don't work or make their clothing, yet Solomon in all his glory was not dressed as beautifully as they are. And if God cares so wonderfully for wildflowers that are here today and thrown into the fire tomorrow, he will certainly care for you. Why do you have so little faith? So don't worry about these things, saying, 'What will we eat? What will we drink? What will we wear?' These things dominate the thoughts of unbelievers, but your heavenly Father already knows all your needs. Seek the Kingdom of God above all else, and live righteously, and he will give you everything you need. So don't worry about tomorrow, for tomorrow will bring its own worries. Today's trouble is enough for today."
> Matthew 6:25-34 (NLT)

> "The LORD is my strength and shield. I trust him with all my heart.
> He helps me, and my heart is filled with joy.
> I burst out in songs of thanksgiving."
> Psalm 28:7 (NLT)

> "Those who know your name trust in you, for you, O LORD,
> do not abandon those who search for you."
> Psalm 9:10 (NLT)

"I pray that God, the source of hope, will fill you completely with joy and peace because you trust in him. Then you will overflow with confident hope through the power of the Holy Spirit."
Romans 15:13 (NLT)

"They do not fear bad news; they confidently trust the LORD to care for them."
Psalm 112:7 (NLT)

"You will keep in perfect peace all who trust in you, all whose thoughts are fixed on you!"
Isaiah 26:3 (NLT)

"Commit everything you do to the LORD. Trust him, and he will help you."
Psalm 37:5 (NLT)

"But blessed are those who trust in the LORD and have made the LORD their hope and confidence. They are like trees planted along a riverbank, with roots that reach deep into the water. Such trees are not bothered by the heat or worried by long months of drought. Their leaves stay green, and they never stop producing fruit."
Jeremiah 17:7-8 (NLT)

"Let me hear of your unfailing love each morning, for I am trusting you. Show me where to walk, for I give myself to you."
Psalm 143:8 (NLT)

"Fearing people is a dangerous trap, but trusting the LORD means safety."
Proverbs 29:25 (NLT)

"Enter into His gates with thanksgiving, and into His courts with praise. Be thankful to Him, and bless His name. For the LORD is good; His mercy is everlasting, and His truth endures to all generations."
Psalm 100:4-5

Thank You Jesus today for...

_____
_____
_____
_____
_____
_____
_____
_____
_____
_____
_____
_____
_____
_____
_____
_____
_____
_____
_____
_____
_____
_____
_____
_____
_____
_____
_____
_____
_____

Day 8
Magnify!
His Word

Almost every time that we hop into the car as a family we talk about what God ministered to our hearts through the Word that day. In the midst of a chaotic schedule it's just an easy habit for us to remember, and it's our version of living out Deuteronomy 6 by talking about the Word of God as we're on our way! We read the One Year Bible as a family. It's been a great tool for discipleship and a perfect way to take in the "Whole counsel of God" regularly. And as a parent, I can't tell you how many times God's Word has spoken to my kids and convicted their hearts over areas of concern that I had been praying about. One day in particular, we were driving, and my son had been in trouble for something the day before. The Proverb for the day addressed his exact cause of punishment, and I wondered if he had noticed. I asked him what God had spoken to him that day and I'll never forget him saying, "I just can't believe that thousands of years ago Solomon wrote these words, and that God had them put in the exact place in the One Year Bible that I would be reading today! I guess God really wanted me to understand why it's wrong." I was so astounded that I almost had to pull my car over! The fact that God not only sets His living Words aflame in our hearts, but then ordains the exact time that we read them amazes me always. Truly His Word is living and powerful!

"As Jesus and the disciples continued on their way to Jerusalem, they came to a certain village where a woman named Martha welcomed him into her home. Her sister, Mary, sat at the Lord's feet, listening to what he taught. But Martha was distracted by the big dinner she was preparing. She came to Jesus and said, 'Lord, doesn't it seem unfair to you that my sister just sits here while I do all the work? Tell her to come and help me.' But the Lord said to her, 'My dear Martha, you are worried and upset over all these details! There is only one thing worth being concerned about. Mary has discovered it, and it will not be taken away from her.'"
Luke 10:38-42 (NLT)

This life worries and troubles us over many things. The daily tasks get in the way of us being able to spend as much time at the feet of Jesus as we would like. If you're anything like me, this passage in Luke can sometimes cause me to question the 'how' of carrying this out. Am I supposed to never accomplish anything and just stay at the feet of Jesus all day? If Martha had done that too, then who would have made dinner? How would they have eaten? If I stop serving and just listen, who will do all that I do? These are all valid questions, but I think they misunderstand the point that Jesus was trying to make. This wasn't a command to stop serving. It was a call to take note of our priorities. I hear people speak often of wanting to read the Bible, but not having time. When something is important to us we find a way to get it done, don't we? I've never ran out of time and had to leave my house for the day in my jammies. Why? Because getting dressed before I leave is important to me! For Martha, yes, dinner needed to be made, but listening to the Words of Jesus could have happened first. Priorities get done. I know we're busy, but I think we might not be as busy as we think we are. It's amazing how we can find time to scroll through social media in order to see insignificant things like what people are eating and where they're vacationing, or check emails daily for coupons and deals, but still not have "time" to read the life-changing Word of God. Job described the Word of God as more important than his daily food. It was a priority to him! When my kids were babies and toddlers I struggled with reading the Bible daily, and this was the verse that God put on my heart. I wanted the Word of God to be more important to me than my daily food as well, so I committed daily to not eat a bite of food until I had "eaten" the Word of God. It's amazing how fast priorities can shift with the right disciplines in place!

We find in John 8 that freedom comes from keeping the Word of God. 1 John tells us that God's commandments ARE His love. Even as a loving mother commands a small child not to touch a hot stove, the most loving thing that God can give to us each day are the instructions from His living Word. The mom's command is not meant to be restrictive or harsh, whether the child finds it difficult to obey or not. The command comes from the heart of love that desires the child to be blessed and unharmed, and the same goes with the Word of God.

The Word of God is living and powerful. Day after day I come to it ready to receive, and I always find it to be all I need. I can't tell you how many times I have come to God's Word with a heavy heart or apprehension of the day ahead, and found His Words to be the soothing balm to my anxious mind or the exact wisdom and direction that I have needed. The Word of God is not outdated, antiquated, expired, or irrelevant. It is the living, powerful Word of God that is sharper than any two-edged sword and able to divide between all that needs dividing. It's a scalpel knife to our souls, cutting away the rotting flesh that will infiltrate our healthy, vibrant spirits. Luke 19 describes the hearers of Jesus as, "hanging on His every Word." One thing is needed. One thing is good. Let's be those who are found hanging upon that alone!

"Evening and morning and at noon I will pray, and cry aloud, and He shall hear my voice."
Psalm 55:17

Magnify!
His Word

"For the word of God is alive and powerful. It is sharper than the sharpest two-edged sword, cutting between soul and spirit, between joint and marrow. It exposes our innermost thoughts and desires."
Hebrews 4:12 (NLT)

"Your word is a lamp to my feet and a light to my path."
Psalm 119:105

"You have been taught the holy Scriptures from childhood, and they have given you the wisdom to receive the salvation that comes by trusting in Christ Jesus. All Scripture is inspired by God and is useful to teach us what is true and to make us realize what is wrong in our lives. It corrects us when we are wrong and teaches us to do what is right. God uses it to prepare and equip his people to do every good work."
2 Timothy 3:15-17 (NLT)

"For the word of the LORD is right and true;
he is faithful in all he does."
Psalm 33:4 (NIV)

"So get rid of all the filth and evil in your lives, and humbly
Accept the word God has planted in your hearts,
for it has the power to save your souls."
James 1:21 (NLT)

"It is the same with my word. I send it out, and it always
produces fruit. It will accomplish all I want it to,
and it will prosper everywhere I send it."
Isaiah 55:11 (NLT)

"The unfolding of your words gives light;
it gives understanding to the simple."
Psalm 119:130 (NIV)

"Then Jesus said to those Jews who believed Him, 'If you abide in My word, you are My disciples indeed. And you shall know the truth, and the truth shall make you free.'"
John 8:31-32

"Whoever despises the word brings destruction on himself, but he who reveres the commandment will be rewarded."
Proverbs 13:13 (ESV)

"Therefore, laying aside all malice, all deceit, hypocrisy, envy, and all evil speaking, as newborn babes, desire the pure milk of the word, that you may grow thereby, if indeed you have tasted that the Lord is gracious."
1 Peter 2:1-3

"And you shall remember that the LORD your God led you all the way these forty years in the wilderness, to humble you and test you, to know what was in your heart, whether you would keep His commandments or not. So He humbled you, allowed you to hunger, and fed you with manna which you did not know nor did your fathers know, that He might make you know that man shall not live by bread alone; but man lives by every word that proceeds from the mouth of the LORD. Your garments did not wear out on you, nor did your foot swell these forty years. You should know in your heart that as a man chastens his son, so the LORD your God chastens you."
Deuteronomy 8:2-5

"We know we love God's children if we love God and obey his commandments. Loving God means keeping his commandments, and his commandments are not burdensome."
1 John 5:2-39 (NLT)

"Now that you have purified yourselves by obeying the truth so that you have sincere love for each other, love one another deeply, from the heart. For you have been born again, not of perishable seed, but of imperishable, through the living and enduring word of God. For, 'All people are like grass, and all their glory is like the flowers of the field; the grass withers and the flowers fall, but the word of the Lord endures forever.' And this is the word that was preached to you."
1 Peter 1:22-25 (NIV)

"Enter into His gates with thanksgiving, and into His courts with praise. Be thankful to Him, and bless His name. For the LORD is good; His mercy is everlasting, and His truth endures to all generations."
Psalm 100:4-5

Thank You Jesus today for...

_____
_____
_____
_____
_____
_____
_____
_____
_____
_____
_____
_____
_____
_____
_____
_____
_____
_____
_____
_____
_____
_____
_____
_____
_____
_____
_____
_____
_____
_____

Day 9
Magnify!
The Father

When my kids were little, the most exciting part of their day was when their father would walk through the front door after a long day at work. "DADDY!!!" was the resounding scream as the chaos of everyone running toward the door ensued. Even the dog would bark excitedly, as if to be screaming, "Daddy is here!" They would all race toward Jason and jump into his arms as fast as their tiny legs could leap. As the children of God, we have the glorious privilege of jumping into the arms of our Heavenly Father each day as well. We find joy in His arms, protection in His strength, and love in His face. Our Heavenly Father's thoughts are continually toward His children with love, grace, care, and provision.

> "For all who are led by the Spirit of God are
> children of God. So you have not received a
> spirit that makes you fearful slaves.
> Instead, you received God's Spirit when he
> adopted you as his own children.
> Now we call him, "Abba, Father."
> For his Spirit joins with our spirit to affirm that
> we are God's children. And since we are his children,
> we are his heirs. In fact, together with Christ
> we are heirs of God's glory."
> Romans 8:14-17 (NLT)

I was blessed to grow up with one of the world's greatest dad's, and I've had the amazing joy of watching my husband fill the shoes of a wonderful earthly father as well. My heart breaks when I have conversations with those who have difficulty relating to God as their Father because of the tragic experiences they've had with their own earthly fathers. If you grew up with a father who has greatly marred your perception of a good dad, I'm so sorry. I don't want to minimize the pain that an upbringing like that can cause. I'm not here to make your perception seem trite, but rather to encourage every heart that God can fill every father void that is left by the scars this world can give. You haven't been given the spirit of slavery or fear, and God isn't limited as a Father from voids left by earthly dads. If anything, the pain left by an earthly father can enhance everything good that the Heavenly Father is. God can be every ounce of the Good Father that your earthly dad was not. The beauty of our Heavenly Father is that He can fill every void that was made, heal every hurt that was given, and renew every heart that was torn. Our Heavenly Father is ever present, always attentive, always protective, always loving, never critical, never disappointed, and never demanding, angry, calloused, or punitive. From the greatest earthly dad to the worst, every single one falls short in some way because humans were never intended to measure up to the perfection of Father God! The fulness of the imperfections found in earthly fathers is erased in our Heavenly Father. Earthly fathers were never meant to satisfy us, complete us, or fill some craving for love, affection, or admiration. Those cravings are meant to be filled in God our Father alone.

Earthly fathers stand as representatives of the relationship, but the fullness of the father figure can only be found in God. God the Father is the only One who protects perfectly. God the Father is the only One who loves completely. God the Father is the only One who is our ever-present help in time of need. All that we seek is found in Him. Maybe we should spend some time in prayer today, asking the perfect Father if there is a way that we perceive Him wrongly based on an earthly view of a messed-up dad. Your heavenly Father longs to scoop you up in His life-giving, comfort giving, ever attentive, and always loving arms! You are the heir of your Heavenly Father. All that He has belongs to you, all that you desire is found in Him alone, and His goodness ever flows toward you.

As my kids got older the screaming sound of "DADDY!" turned into, "Hey Dad," with a little less enthusiasm. I know it's a natural part of the earthly home, but matured distance isn't to be a part of our story with the heavenly Father. Our heavenly Father still longs for us to run to Him as a small child runs to their father, with just as much enthusiasm, need, desire, and love. When I was little, my dad used to put my feet on top of his and we would dance around the living room. He would sing songs to me while we danced, and I loved being in his arms, moving wherever he was taking me. Whether you're feeling a bit far from the Heavenly Father today or not, let's hop up on top of His feet for a little spiritual dancing! Let's take some time to draw near to our Dad, imagining ourselves running to Him and crying out, "Abba Father!" This Dad will never fail us or fall short, He's always bigger than us, always greater than us, and He has all we're seeking from a true Father relationship. Let Him scoop you up in His arms of love today.

*"Evening and morning and at noon I will pray, and cry aloud,
and He shall hear my voice."*
Psalm 55:17

Magnify!
The Father

"Father to the fatherless, defender of widows— this is God,
whose dwelling is holy. God places the lonely in families;
he sets the prisoners free and gives them joy.
But he makes the rebellious live in a sun-scorched land."
Psalm 68:5-6 (NLT)

"But for us, there is one God, the Father, by whom all things were created, and for whom we live. And there is one Lord, Jesus Christ, through whom all things were created, and through whom we live."
1 Corinthians 8:6 (NLT)

"But now, O LORD, You are our Father;
We are the clay, and You our potter;
And all we are the work of Your hand."
Isaiah 64:8

"Whatever is good and perfect is a gift coming down to us from God our Father, who created all the lights in the heavens.
He never changes or casts a shifting shadow."
James 1:17 (NLT)

"As a father has compassion on his children, so the LORD has
compassion on those who fear him"
Psalm 103:13 (NIV)

"Blessed be the God and Father of our Lord Jesus Christ, who has blessed us with every spiritual blessing in the heavenly places in Christ"
Ephesians 1:3

"My child, don't reject the LORD's discipline, and don't be upset when he corrects you. For the LORD corrects those he loves,
just as a father corrects a child in whom he delights."
Proverbs 3:11-12 (NLT)

"And he arose and came to his father. But when he was still a great way off, his father saw him and had compassion, and ran and fell on his neck and kissed him. And the son said to him, 'Father, I have sinned against heaven and in your sight, and am no longer worthy to be called your son.' But the father said to his servants, 'Bring out the best robe and put it on him, and put a ring on his hand and sandals on his feet. And bring the fatted calf here and kill it, and let us eat and be merry; for this my son was dead and is alive again; he was lost and is found.'
And they began to be merry."
Luke 15:20-24

"Jesus told him, "I am the way, the truth, and the life. No one can come to the Father except through me. If you had really known me, you would know who my Father is. From now on, you do know him and have seen him!" Philip said, "Lord, show us the Father, and we will be satisfied." Jesus replied, "Have I been with you all this time, Philip, and yet you still don't know who I am? Anyone who has seen me has seen the Father! So why are you asking me to show him to you? Don't you believe that I am in the Father and the Father is in me? The words I speak are not my own, but my Father who lives in me does his work through me. Just believe that I am in the Father and the Father is in me. Or at least believe because of the work you have seen me do. I tell you the truth, anyone who believes in me will do the same works I have done, and even greater works, because I am going to be with the Father. You can ask for anything in my name, and I will do it,
so that the Son can bring glory to the Father.
Yes, ask me for anything in my name, and I will do it!"
John 14:6-12 (NLT)

"LORD, look down from heaven; look from your holy, glorious home, and see us. Where is the passion and the might you used to show on our behalf? Where are your mercy and compassion now? Surely you are still our Father! Even if Abraham and Jacob would disown us, LORD, you would still be our Father. you are our Redeemer from ages past."
Isaiah 63:15-16 (NLT)

"See how very much our Father loves us,
for he calls us his children,
and that is what we are!"
1 John 3:1 (NLT)

"Enter into His gates with thanksgiving, and into His courts with praise. Be thankful to Him, and bless His name. For the LORD is good; His mercy is everlasting, and His truth endures to all generations."
Psalm 100:4-5

Thank You Jesus today for…

_____
_____
_____
_____
_____
_____
_____
_____
_____
_____
_____
_____
_____
_____
_____
_____
_____
_____
_____
_____
_____
_____
_____
_____
_____
_____
_____
_____
_____

Day 10
Magnify!
Our Shield

Like most kids, I was terrified of the dark when I was a little girl. I remember lying in bed at night, just sure that every lurking shadow was a monster or an alien about to pop out of its hiding place and drag me away to some unknown lair to devour me. I have memories of fear, terror, tears, and panic. I have memories of calling out to my parents who graciously got out of bed to come sit with me in the dark until I fell asleep again. One night in particular, though, I have a memory of such peace in the midst of the fear. My parents prayed over me every night, and this night was no different. But this night I have a distinct memory of Jesus whispering in my ear that He was my shield. He gave me the picture in my heart of Him like an impenetrable force, setting Himself over my bed and all around me like a solid wall. He told me that nothing could reach me because He was covering me completely. Each night after that, I would start to fear what was all around me, but suddenly I would think of the picture that Jesus had given me in my heart, and my fear was eased. I would imagine that God was around me like a shield, covering every square inch of my mattress, with me tucked safely within Him, and I would find myself falling asleep in the peace of His refuge. There is still such truth and peace found in that beautiful picture Jesus gave me so long ago. Of course, I'm no longer afraid of monsters, but monstrous terror can still rise up in my heart. We live in an unsettled world, but with God as our shield we have nothing to fear.

> "But let all who take refuge in you rejoice; let them sing joyful praises forever. Spread your protection over them,
> that all who love your name may be filled with joy.
> For you bless the godly, O LORD;
> you surround them with your shield of love."
> Psalm 5:11-12 (NLT)

As children of God, living shielded by His loving care is our daily reality. We can rejoice because we are covered and surrounded. His love is ever upon us, ever around us, ever beside us, and ever within us. The shield of God is stronger than the strongest of shields. As those who take refuge in God, we don't find peace and safety in walls, locked doors, or the most solid barracks. A mighty fortress is our God, and He is the shield that surrounds us and keeps us safe! There is no peace like the heart that knows it is kept within the loving care of the God who surrounds us with His shield of might. We can look up, filled with confidence, flooded with boldness, and fired up with passion because not a single hair of our head will fall without the sovereign knowledge of our good God allowing it for His loving purposes. Being shielded by God's love doesn't mean that our lives won't ever be touched by tragedy or trial, but it does mean that not one fiery dart from the enemy will be able to penetrate into our lives that God doesn't welcome in by His plans of using that dart for strengthening, for growth, and to further form us into His image and develop within us a heart after His glory.

We are told in Ephesians 6 to take up our shields of faith. We are to have faith by believing that God truly is the shield about us that He says He is. We have faith in the truth that God is who He says He is and will do what He says He will do. Taking up the shield of faith is believing that God will always be watching us and guarding us with His loving hand. Taking up the shield of faith is trusting that God's care will surround us for all of our days; and we will only walk through what has been strength tested specifically for us, for that day, for that time, by the gracious, loving hand of God.

In 2 Kings 11 we read of a wicked grandma raising herself up as the queen and securing her throne by killing her own grandchildren. Long story short, one of her grandsons was secretly whisked away to safety and was hidden away in the temple of the LORD for six years. When the priest decided it was time for Joash to be made king, he gave the command for the guards to completely surround young king Joash with weapons in hand. They were instructed to stay close to the king wherever he went, until he was led to the throne in safety. You and I live like this king. We have this same beautiful protection, but even better! Ours is not just the fleeting, and at times, failing protection of human flesh. We have God as the shield about us. Wherever we go, God our Shield surrounds us in protection, love, and care, leading us to His eternal throne room.

Knowing that God is our Shield gives us confidence to be able to walk out the calling that He gives to us. When we go out into the world under the obedience of the One who is calling us, there is a special protection about us. We are protected as we speak His messages of truth. We can have confidence in troubles, in wars, and in ruin. We have confidence that we are always under the careful eye of the One who promises that if His eye is on the sparrow, how much more is He watching over us? We have the sovereign love and care of God, our Shield about us, and we can find rest, hope, peace, and blessings in that solid truth.

"Evening and morning and at noon I will pray, and cry aloud, and He shall hear my voice."
Psalm 55:17

Magnify!
Our Shield

"Every word of God proves true;
he is a shield to those who take refuge in him."
Proverbs 30:5 (NLT)

"He will cover you with his feathers, and under his wings you will find refuge; his faithfulness will be your shield and rampart."
Psalm 91:4 (NIV)

"I love you, LORD; you are my strength. The LORD is my rock, my fortress, and my savior; my God is my rock, in whom I find protection. He is my shield, the power that saves me, and my place of safety."
Psalm 18:1-2 (NLT)

"the word of the LORD came to Abram in a vision: 'Do not be afraid, Abram. I am your shield, your very great reward."
Genesis 15:1 (NIV)

"But You, O LORD, are a shield for me,
My glory and the One who lifts up my head."
Psalm 3:3

"He is my steadfast love and my fortress, my stronghold and my deliverer, my shield and he in whom I take refuge, who subdues peoples under me."
Psalm 144:2 (ESV)

"We wait in hope for the LORD; he is our help and our shield."
Psalm 33:20 (NIV)

"For the LORD God is our sun and our shield. He gives us grace and
glory. The LORD will withhold no good thing
from those who do what is right."
Psalm 84:11 (NLT)

"You are my hiding place and my shield;
I hope in Your word."
Psalm 119:114

"above all, taking the shield of faith with which you will be able to
quench all the fiery darts of the wicked one."
Ephesians 6:16

"David sang this song to the LORD on the day the LORD rescued him
from all his enemies and from Saul. He sang: 'The LORD is my rock, my
fortress, and my savior; my God is my rock, in whom I find protection.
He is my shield, the power that saves me, and my place of safety.
He is my refuge, my savior, the one who saves me from violence.
I called on the LORD, who is worthy of praise,
and he saved me from my enemies.'"
2 Samuel 22:1-4 (NLT)

"O Israel, trust in the LORD; He is their help and their shield.
O house of Aaron, trust in the LORD; He is their help and their shield.
You who fear the LORD, trust in the LORD,
He is their help and their shield."
Psalm 115:9-11

"How blessed you are, O Israel!
Who else is like you, a people saved by the LORD?
He is your protecting shield and your triumphant sword!
Your enemies will cringe before you, and you will stomp on their backs!"
Deuteronomy 33:29 (NLT)

"Praise the LORD! For he has heard my cry for mercy.
The LORD is my strength and shield. I trust him with all my heart.
He helps me, and my heart is filled with joy. I burst out in songs of
thanksgiving. The LORD gives his people strength.
He is a safe fortress for his anointed king."
Psalm 28:6-9 (NLT)

"Enter into His gates with thanksgiving, and into His courts with praise. Be thankful to Him, and bless His name. For the LORD is good; His mercy is everlasting, and His truth endures to all generations."
Psalm 100:4-5

Thank You Jesus today for…

_____
_____
_____
_____
_____
_____
_____
_____
_____
_____
_____
_____
_____
_____
_____
_____
_____
_____
_____
_____
_____
_____
_____
_____
_____
_____
_____
_____
_____
_____
_____

Day 11
Magnify!
His Return

Now let me just say right off the bat, (An amazing phrase for an extremely non-sporty person) I'm not here to argue eschatology. Girls with all different types of end times beliefs will be reading this book, and my heart is not to divide us in any way. Though I've got some strong beliefs and opinions, I'm not here to debate anything that could only lead to the offensiveness and distraction of some. My desire for today is to magnify not so much the *when*, but the thought of *how* we're to wait while we wait for the "when" that you interpret Scripture to be talking about. People have been arguing with each other about end times for hundreds upon hundreds of years. Aside from the fact that I don't think we're going to solve the church's problems in a tiny devotional written by an extremely non-scholarly girl, I'd rather focus today on what our lives should look like while we wait. God has called us to wait and watch for Jesus to come in whatever time period it is that you're watching and waiting for. He's called us to have His heart while we wait and His eyes for the lost while we watch. It's the expectant watching and waiting that keeps us on the path expecting the coming of Jesus at any moment!

"Therefore you also be ready, for the Son of Man is coming at an hour you do not expect. Who then is a faithful and wise servant, whom his master made ruler over his household, to give them food in due season? Blessed is that servant whom his master, when he comes, will find so doing. Assuredly, I say to you that he will make him ruler over all his goods. But if that evil servant says in his heart, 'My master is delaying his coming,' and begins to beat his fellow servants, and to eat and drink with the drunkards, the master of that servant will come on a day when he is not looking for him and at an hour that he is not aware of, and will cut him in two and appoint him his portion with the hypocrites.
There shall be weeping and gnashing of teeth."
Matthew 24:44-51

Jesus notes that in the life of humanity, it's the perceived delaying of His coming that keeps us from being the faithful and wise servants we set out to be. Remember in Exodus 32 when Moses was up on the mountain with God? The Israelites came to Aaron with the declaration that Moses had delayed his coming and they didn't know what happened to him. They asked Aaron to make gods that would lead them into the promise land because they didn't even know whether or not Moses was coming back.

The mindset of apathy and rebellion came when the Israelites assumed that the one they had been waiting for was no longer coming back. Knowing the same tendency plagues us as well, Jesus calls us to live with the mindset that we could be face to face with Him at any moment. He reminds us to expect His coming when we least expect His coming! Watching daily for Jesus to return keeps us treating our fellow servants with His gracious love and keeps us pushing forward to the kingdom of God at a steady pace.

Anytime I leave my teenagers at home alone I give them the same exhortation, "I want things clean when I get home!" You who have teens know what it's like to leave a clean house and come home to tornado alley. I have no idea how they can mess up every square inch just within a couple of hours. Wanting not to be the yelling mom upon return, I always "lovingly" remind them to clean up after themselves. Without fail, I get a call or a text before I get home saying, "Mom, when are you coming home so we can make sure the house is clean?" I respond the same every time. "I'm not going to tell you when I'm coming home because I want you to keep the house clean the whole time." Maybe you think I'm a little crazy to expect a clean house in teenage world, but the same principal applies to us as we wait for the Heavenly Kingdom. It's in our human nature to wait until someone important is watching us before we do our best, or to wait until it's crunch time before we give it our all. Knowing that we all have a propensity toward procrastination and apathy, God exhorts us to live as though He could be coming for us at any moment. He reminds us that the constant kind and loving actions toward others comes from thinking that the Master of the House could return home at any moment. A faithful and wise servant lives with the mindset that our lives could suddenly be cut shorter than we expected, and so desires to live to their fullest capacity for Jesus each day. A faithful and wise servant lives to accomplish as much for the kingdom of God as possible each day because they know the Master isn't delaying His coming. A faithful and wise servant treats others with respect because they remember that any moment could be the "blink of an eye" that we see Jesus in.

Jesus is on His way… whatever that looks like to your understanding. He's coming soon! Whether He's coming for the world right now or not, this is still your last generation to live in. Are we ready? Are we watching? Do we have eyes fixed upon the eternal, the heavenly, and the permanent? Do we have shallow roots in this life? Are we busy about the Father's business? We don't know the day or the hour, but I want to be found ready to jump into heaven at any moment, don't you?

"Evening and morning and at noon I will pray, and cry aloud, and He shall hear my voice."
Psalm 55:17

Magnify!
His Return

"But of that day and hour no one knows, not even the angels of heaven, but My Father only. But as the days of Noah were, so also will the coming of the Son of Man be. For as in the days before the flood, they were eating and drinking, marrying and giving in marriage, until the day that Noah entered the ark, and did not know until the flood came and took them all away, so also will the coming of the Son of Man be. Then two men will be in the field: one will be taken and the other left. Two women will be grinding at the mill: one will be taken and the other left. Watch therefore, for you do not know what hour your Lord is coming. But know this, that if the master of the house had known what hour the thief would come, he would have watched and not allowed his house to be broken into. Therefore you also be ready, for the Son of Man is coming at an hour you do not expect."
Matthew 24:36-44

"so also Christ was offered once for all time as a sacrifice to take away the sins of many people. He will come again, not to deal with our sins, but to bring salvation to all who are eagerly waiting for him."
Hebrews 9:28 (NLT)

"But let me reveal to you a wonderful secret. We will not all die, but we will all be transformed! It will happen in a moment, in the blink of an eye, when the last trumpet is blown. For when the trumpet sounds, those who have died will be raised to live forever. And we who are living will also be transformed. For our dying bodies must be transformed into bodies that will never die; our mortal bodies must be transformed into immortal bodies. Then, when our dying bodies have been transformed into bodies that will never die, this Scripture will be fulfilled:
Death is swallowed up in victory. O death, where is your victory? O death, where is your sting?"
1 Corinthians 15:51-55 (NLT)

"Then the Kingdom of Heaven will be like ten bridesmaids who took their lamps and went to meet the bridegroom. Five of them were foolish, and five were wise. The five who were foolish didn't take enough olive oil for their lamps, but the other five were wise enough to take along extra oil. When the bridegroom was delayed, they all became drowsy and fell asleep. At midnight they were roused by the shout, 'Look, the bridegroom is coming! Come out and meet him!' All the bridesmaids got up and prepared their lamps. Then the five foolish ones asked the others, 'Please give us some of your oil because our lamps are going out.' But the others replied, 'We don't have enough for all of us. Go to a shop and buy some for yourselves.' But while they were gone to buy oil, the bridegroom came. Then those who were ready went in with him to the marriage feast, and the door was locked. Later, when the other five bridesmaids returned, they stood outside, calling, 'Lord! Lord! Open the door for us!' But he called back, 'Believe me, I don't know you!' So you, too, must keep watch! For you do not know the day or hour of my return."
Matthew 25:1-13 (NLT)

"There will be signs in the sun, moon and stars. On the earth, nations will be in anguish and perplexity at the roaring and tossing of the sea. People will faint from terror, apprehensive of what is coming on the world, for the heavenly bodies will be shaken. At that time they will see the Son of Man coming in a cloud with power and great glory. When these things begin to take place, stand up and lift up your heads, because your redemption is drawing near."
Luke 21:25-28 (NIV)

"Look, he is coming with the clouds, and every eye will see him, even those who pierced him; and all peoples on earth will mourn because of him. So shall it be! Amen."
Revelation 1:7 (NIV)

"For the Lord Himself will descend from heaven with a shout, with the voice of an archangel, and with the trumpet of God. And the dead in Christ will rise first. Then we who are alive and remain shall be caught up together with them in the clouds to meet the Lord in the air. And thus we shall always be with the Lord.
Therefore comfort one another with these words."
1 Thessalonians 4:16-18

"And behold, I am coming quickly, and My reward is with Me, to give to every one according to his work."
Revelation 22:12

"Enter into His gates with thanksgiving, and into His courts with praise. Be thankful to Him, and bless His name. For the LORD is good; His mercy is everlasting, and His truth endures to all generations."
Psalm 100:4-5

Thank You Jesus today for…

Day 12
Magnify!
Our Provider

So, this story might paint me in an 'awful mom' light, but I hope you can see a picture of Jesus somewhere in it! I have the tendency to be one of those crazy helicopter moms who wants to hover way too close to the needs of her children. One day I was with a group of my friends, silently listening to how all of their kids got up each morning and made their own breakfast. My kids knew how to cook with me because we would do fun, little projects in the kitchen together. But as far as making breakfast by themselves, nope! I was up before them each day cooking, so that they could wake up to a steaming hot breakfast without lifting a finger. One summer morning, after this conversation, I decided to wait until my kids asked for breakfast, just to see what happened. 8 am passed- they said nothing. 9 am passed- they said nothing. Finally, at 9:45 am my oldest daughter who, was around 10 years old at the time said, "My tummy hurts." I looked at her in amazement, realizing that she had never felt hunger before, so she had no idea what it was! She thought the problem was an aching in her tummy, but I knew that her true need was to have some food. (And to be taught how to make her own breakfast!)

> "Keep on asking, and you will receive what you ask for. Keep on seeking, and you will find. Keep on knocking, and the door will be opened to you. For everyone who asks, receives. Everyone who seeks, finds. And to everyone who knocks, the door will be opened. You parents—if your children ask for a loaf of bread, do you give them a stone instead? Or if they ask for a fish, do you give them a snake? Of course not! So if you sinful people know how to give good gifts to your children, how much more will your heavenly Father give good gifts to those who ask him."
> Matthew 7:7-11 (NLT)

Our greatest need is to go to Jesus in prayer, seeking Him for all we need. When we look to God as our Provider we find answers to questions we weren't asking, provisions for needs we didn't know we had, and hope for situations that have yet to arise. Sometimes our lives can look like we have needs that are unmet and unfulfilled, not because we have an inept God, but because we have yet to find out what our greatest need in the moment actually is. God knows the answers to the needs that we don't even know we have yet. He knows every detail that He plans on providing for us as we take each step of faith in obedience. He provides not only what we ask for, but He even tells us through prayer what to ask for because He knows what our greatest needs truly are! The answers to the questions within us are found in looking to Jesus as our Provider. We have not because we ask not. When we're in communion with Him He tells us what to seek, and then we get to sit back and watch Him provide the good gifts that He promises to give. Psalm 37:4 tells us that when we delight ourselves in God, He gives us the desires of our hearts. Not only does He answer our prayers by fulfilling our desires, but as we are delighting in Him and putting our faith and trust in Him as the sovereign Provider, He puts those desires within us that He is already wanting to fulfill!

In John 6 Jesus points out a lack and a need. He anticipates the hunger of those who have been following Him for days, and so He asks His disciples how they can meet the needs of the people before the actual need arises. This sends certain disciples into a frenzy. They immediately forget all they've learned and declare that the people need to be sent away because there is not enough money or food to take care of the needs of each follower. I love thinking about the heart of Jesus as He asked His disciples to feed the multitude. Jesus wasn't actually wondering what to do. Jesus wasn't panicked over the situation, wondering where they could get enough money to feed the hungry people. Jesus knew the Father would provide for the need that had arisen. Rather than sending the disciples into an uptight tizzy, I think Jesus was hoping to hear two simple sentences from them. "What do You think we should do?" And, "How would You like us to do it?" So often Jesus shows us a lack, not because He wants to send us into a desperate, uptight, nervous fit, but because He wants us to look to Him as the Provider who already has the perfect plan in place. We just need to seek Him for the details. Jesus already knows the miraculous ways He wants to provide, but He shows us the void and the lack so that we will have to look to Him in prayer. He wants us to ask, to seek, and to knock; not to wonder, to flip out, and panic! Jesus wants us to see the need, the void, the lack, and the impossibilities so that He can remind us that He's the Provider God and isn't limited by our human limitations. At the end of this moment of obedience in John 6, the disciples had baskets of leftovers, full tummies, and a new awe of the miraculous Provider. Jehovah Jireh, our Provider is not limited to physical needs. He is our ever-present Help in time of need. When we need patience, He has unlimited patience for us. When we are in need of comfort, grace, a place to hide, or endless strength, He has all we need for every moment.

What do we need? What do we desire? What do we lack? Have we asked? Maybe it's a good day to spend some time praying to the One who has promised to provide for every need as we ask, seek, and knock upon the door of His heart!

"Evening and morning and at noon I will pray, and cry aloud, and He shall hear my voice."
Psalm 55:17

Magnify!
Our Provider

"And this same God who takes care of me will supply all your needs from his glorious riches, which have been given to us in Christ Jesus. Now all glory to God our Father forever and ever! Amen."
Philippians 4:19-20 (NLT)

"The LORD is my shepherd; I have all that I need. He lets me rest in green meadows; he leads me beside peaceful streams. He renews my strength. He guides me along right paths, bringing honor to his name. Even when I walk through the darkest valley, I will not be afraid, for you are close beside me. Your rod and your staff protect and comfort me. You prepare a feast for me in the presence of my enemies. You honor me by anointing my head with oil. My cup overflows with blessings. Surely your goodness and unfailing love will pursue me all the days of my life, and I will live in the house of the LORD forever."
Psalm 23:1-6 (NLT)

"Every good gift and every perfect gift is from above, and comes down from the Father of lights, with whom there is no variation or shadow of turning."
James 1:17

"Then Jesus told them, "I tell you the truth, if you have faith and don't doubt, you can do things like this and much more. You can even say to this mountain, 'May you be lifted up and thrown into the sea,' and it will happen. You can pray for anything, and if you have faith, you will receive it."
Matthew 21:21 (NLT)

"Remember this—a farmer who plants only a few seeds will get a small crop. But the one who plants generously will get a generous crop. You must each decide in your heart how much to give. And don't give reluctantly or in response to pressure. "For God loves a person who gives cheerfully." And God will generously provide all you need. Then you will always have everything you need and plenty left over to share with others. As the Scriptures say, "They share freely and give generously to the poor. Their good deeds will be remembered forever." For God is the one who provides seed for the farmer and then bread to eat. In the same way, he will provide and increase your resources and then produce a great harvest of generosity in you. Yes, you will be enriched in every way so that you can always be generous."
2 Corinthians 9:6-11 (NLT)

"Fear the LORD, you his holy people, for those who fear him lack nothing. The lions may grow weak and hungry,
but those who seek the LORD lack no good thing."
Psalm 34:9-10 (NIV)

"Therefore I tell you, do not worry about your life, what you will eat or drink; or about your body, what you will wear. Is not life more than food, and the body more than clothes? Look at the birds of the air; they do not sow or reap or store away in barns, and yet your heavenly Father feeds them. Are you not much more valuable than they? Can any one of you by worrying add a single hour to your life? And why do you worry about clothes? See how the flowers of the field grow. They do not labor or spin. Yet I tell you that not even Solomon in all his splendor was dressed like one of these. If that is how God clothes the grass of the field, which is here today and tomorrow is thrown into the fire, will he not much more clothe you—you of little faith? So do not worry, saying, 'What shall we eat?' or 'What shall we drink?' or 'What shall we wear?' For the pagans run after all these things, and your heavenly Father knows that you need them. But seek first his kingdom and his righteousness, and all these things will be given to you as well."
Matthew 6:25-33 (NIV)

"For the LORD God is our sun and our shield. He gives us grace and glory. The LORD will withhold no good thing from
those who do what is right."
Psalm 84:11 (NLT)

"Enter into His gates with thanksgiving, and into His courts with praise. Be thankful to Him, and bless His name. For the LORD is good; His mercy is everlasting, and His truth endures to all generations."
Psalm 100:4-5

Thank You Jesus today for…

_____
_____
_____
_____
_____
_____
_____
_____
_____
_____
_____
_____
_____
_____
_____
_____
_____
_____
_____
_____
_____
_____
_____
_____
_____
_____
_____
_____
_____

Day 13
Magnify!
Love

"God is love"... what does that sentence do to your heart? What does it say to your soul? What feelings does it ignite within you? Really stop and think about it. Every good thing that is experienced, every Holy thing that is known, every pleasing thing that is out there, and every beautiful thing that is available is all wrapped up in love; and this love is the very epitome of who God is. God IS love. He doesn't just create love, give love, know love, or extend love. He IS love. There is no love without God and there is no God without love. He breathes out love, He exudes love, He speaks love, He *IS* love. I don't know that we will ever be able to wrap our finite brains around all that He is, or all of the love that He gives. Remember in Exodus 34 when Moses asks just to see a glimpse of God's glory? As God passed before Moses, it was His love that He declared, because His love IS His glory. Love is who God is. Love IS always found in the Presence of God, because Love IS God's Presence.

> "This is real love- not that we loved God, but that he loved us and sent his Son as a sacrifice to take away our sins... We know how much God loves us, and we have put our trust in his love. God is love, and all who live in love live in God, and God lives in them. And as we live in God, our love grows more perfect.... Such love has no fear, because perfect love expels all fear. If we are afraid, it is for fear of punishment, and this shows that we have not fully experienced his perfect love."
> 1 John 4 (NLT)

Have you ever seen someone who looked perfectly and beautifully loved? Have you seen the confidence that being loved gives to their countenance? Maybe you've sat with newlyweds or an engaged couple, and they can't take their eyes off of each other. Whether you have this type of earthly physical love or not, the most amazing truth we will ever hear is that this is the kind of love that Jesus feels toward us! You are so fully loved by God that He was willing to give up everything to obtain your heart. He knew that there was no way to a holy and eternal relationship with Him apart from the cross, so with His heart set upon you, He sacrificed Himself in love. Perfect love casts out all fear, because if we truly understood how God looks at us, feels about us, desires us, and longs for us, we would never have another insecure or fearful moment ever again. To know and remember that we are loved perfectly should change the way that we feel about ourselves and our past forever. The perfect sacrifice of Jesus on the cross, that glorious love displayed, and our eternal destination as the fully loved bride of Christ should keep us from feeling as though we ever need the love of anyone else to be complete. It's not that earthly relationships aren't to be had, it's just that they can't ever fulfill us in the way that God's love was designed to fulfill us. The perfect love of God changes who we are forever. His perfect love upon us is the end of worldly descriptions such as forsaken, forgotten, abandoned, alone, betrayed, left out, lonely, and lost. To be fully loved changes our identity from loser to victor, from outcast to belonging, from shameful to beautiful, from stained to pure, and from unwanted to highly desired. We have gone from being disregarded by those in the world to being those who are highly regarded by a King; and not just any king. We are highly regarded, perfectly loved, and greatly desired by the King of kings and Lord of lords. Yours is a desired love in His eyes, and His loving gaze is set upon you forever. You are seen, not in anger, annoyance, or ugliness, but seen by the greatest eyes of love that we could ever imagine. Have you ever been overwhelmed by a gaze of love? Could we see the face of Jesus with our physical eyes, I think His love in its fullness would overwhelm us beyond capacity. Just feeling a drop more than His regular love has overwhelmed me at times- hasn't it you? Let's pray today to be overwhelmed by the poured-out love of our Savior! Our lives are never the same after tasting just a drop more than the regular dose. Our thirst and hunger for more of that love we've experienced exceeds all thirsts, desire, satisfaction, and fulfillment for the rest of our days!

It's Valentine's Day as I write this, and it has me wondering why we associate the color red with the deepest of loves: red roses, red hearts, red balloons. Could it be that our Beloved put that color in our world as a mark of the truest, purest, and deepest love because it was that color of red that marked His truest, purest, and deepest love for us? It was the red of His cleansing, healing, sanctifying, and saving blood that rushed down from the cross to save us with His sacrificial love. It was the deep red of the blood of Jesus, testifying that His words of love were backed up by the most saving action that has ever taken place. God's words are not empty words of love found on a card, but words that have the weight and heft of actions behind them. There are no empty promises with our God's love, and no wonder of how long it will last. His love is shown by promises fulfilled and backed by a greater weight of value than all the gold or chocolate in the world. Every day is Valentine's Day with the One who promises in His love to never forsake us, but to be with us always.

"Evening and morning and at noon I will pray, and cry aloud, and He shall hear my voice."
Psalm 55:17

Magnify!
Love

"Behold what manner of love the Father has bestowed on us, that we should be called children of God!"
1 John 3:1

"The LORD appeared to us in the past, saying: 'I have loved you with an everlasting love; I have drawn you with unfailing kindness.'"
Jeremiah 31:3 (NIV)

"For God so loved the world that he gave his one and only Son, that whoever believes in him shall not perish but have eternal life."
John 3:16 (NIV)

"Give thanks to the God of heaven,
for his steadfast love endures forever."
Psalm 136:26 (ESV)

"But God demonstrates His own love toward us, in that while we were still sinners, Christ died for us."
Romans 5:8

"For a brief moment I abandoned you, but with great compassion I will take you back. In a burst of anger I turned my face away for a little while. But with everlasting love I will have compassion on you," says the LORD, your Redeemer. "Just as I swore in the time of Noah that I would never again let a flood cover the earth, so now I swear that I will never again be angry and punish you. For the mountains may move and the hills disappear, but even then my faithful love for you will remain. My covenant of blessing will never be broken,"
says the LORD, who has mercy on you."
Isaiah 54:7-10 (NLT)

"The LORD your God in your midst, The Mighty One, will save; He will rejoice over you with gladness, He will quiet you with His love, He will rejoice over you with singing."
Zephaniah 3:17

"But God is so rich in mercy, and he loved us so much, that even though we were dead because of our sins, he gave us life when he raised Christ from the dead. (It is only by God's grace that you have been saved!)"
Ephesians 2:4-5 (NLT)

"But you, O Lord, are a God of compassion and mercy, slow to get angry and filled with unfailing love and faithfulness."
Psalm 86:15 (NLT)

"The LORD did not set his heart on you and choose you because you were more numerous than other nations, for you were the smallest of all nations! Rather, it was simply that the LORD loves you, and he was keeping the oath he had sworn to your ancestors. That is why the LORD rescued you with such a strong hand from your slavery and from the oppressive hand of Pharaoh, king of Egypt. Understand, therefore, that the LORD your God is indeed God. He is the faithful God who keeps his covenant for a thousand generations and lavishes his unfailing love on those who love him and obey his commands."
Deuteronomy 7:7-9 (NLT)

"Can anything ever separate us from Christ's love? Does it mean he no longer loves us if we have trouble or calamity, or are persecuted, or hungry, or destitute, or in danger, or threatened with death? (As the Scriptures say, "For your sake we are killed every day; we are being slaughtered like sheep.") No, despite all these things, overwhelming victory is ours through Christ, who loved us. And I am convinced that nothing can ever separate us from God's love. Neither death nor life, neither angels nor demons, neither our fears for today nor our worries about tomorrow—not even the powers of hell can separate us from God's love. No power in the sky above or in the earth below—indeed, nothing in all creation will ever be able to separate us from the love of God that is revealed in Christ Jesus our Lord."
Romans 8:35-39 (NLT)

"Enter into His gates with thanksgiving, and into His courts with praise. Be thankful to Him, and bless His name. For the LORD is good; His mercy is everlasting, and His truth endures to all generations."
Psalm 100:4-5

Thank You Jesus today for…

_____
_____
_____
_____
_____
_____
_____
_____
_____
_____
_____
_____
_____
_____
_____
_____
_____
_____
_____
_____
_____
_____
_____
_____
_____
_____
_____
_____
_____

Day 14
Magnify!
The Good Shepherd

So, we've all heard the stories of how scatterbrained and inept sheep are, right? Yet over and over in Scripture we humans are compared to sheep. While some take offense at this, I say, "Yes and Amen!" I'm completely incapable and inept all by myself. I choose wrong, think wrong, decide wrong, and just plain AM wrong most of the time. Left to my own devices I can mess up a job, a relationship, a teaching, a calling, a kid, a conversation, and a counseling appointment in a record amount of time. I don't take offense to the label of a sheep. I admit readily that without the Good Shepherd in my life I would be hopelessly and endlessly lost! On my own I feel discontented, fretful, weak, lost, and alone. Praise God we have the Good Shepherd who daily is available to shepherd, guide, and meet all of our known and unknown needs.

> "The LORD is my shepherd; I have all that I need.
> He lets me rest in green meadows; he leads me beside peaceful streams.
> He renews my strength. He guides me along right paths,
> bringing honor to his name. Even when I walk through the darkest
> valley, I will not be afraid, for you are close beside me. Your rod and
> your staff protect and comfort me. You prepare a feast for me
> in the presence of my enemies. You honor me by anointing my head
> with oil. My cup overflows with blessings. Surely your goodness and
> unfailing love will pursue me all the days of my life,
> and I will live in the house of the LORD forever."
> Psalm 23 (NLT)

Shepherds have an endless amount of work to do when it comes to caring for their sheep, and our Good Shepherd's job description is no different. Left alone sheep will topple over, unable to get up on their own, eventually succumbing to death on their backs. Without oil poured over them, sheep will headbutt each other, causing serious damage to themselves. Without a shepherd to guide them along the paths, sheep will eat grass down to the roots and die in a barren field, though a field full of grass is just a little farther down the road. Without a shepherd, sheep will follow each other off the edge of a cliff and fall to their demise. Without a shepherd's careful watch, sheep will wander off and get lost, unable to find their way home. Without a shepherd to watch over them sheep are exposed and vulnerable to wild animals and other terrifying situations that can lead to heart-attacks and death. Without a shepherd finding still water for the sheep to drink, they will die of dehydration rather than take the "frightening" risk of drinking from moving water.

I don't know about you, but without my Good Shepherd I can cry out, "Same!" to every one of those situations. I too have fallen into sin, stumbled over my own words, and have found myself unable to rise out of a crumpled heap on my own. It's in those times that I have found my Good Shepherd's tender hands gently giving me strength and enabling me to rise up on His wings. I too have run angry toward other sheep, not realizing the damage that I am doing through my careless temper. It's in those times I have found the soothing oil of the Holy Spirit poured upon my hot head, calming me down by His kind graciousness. I too have tasted of the dirt of this world, unable to find the nutritious growth that I seek. It's in those times that my Good Shepherd has pulled the roots of this world away from me and led me to feast in satisfaction on that which I unknowingly sought. I too have followed and led other sheep off the cliffs of immorality, unedifying conversations, covetous desires, and mindless pursuits. I too have plunged off of more than one cliff that has been the momentary death of my spiritual maturity. In those times my Good Shepherd has caught me and held me close to His heart while I healed from the deep wounds of a lesson learned. I too have wandered away from the sheepfold and have discovered the enemy to be the prowling and roaring lion that the Bible describes. In those times I have found the Good Shepherd strong, sure, and steadfast as He fought the battles with the enemy that I could never win. He has restored me to His fold, bandaged my wounds, and brought safety to the fear. I too have felt the lack of peace that comes from the wild animals of the world that sought to steal, kill, and destroy every good work that God was doing in my heart. In those times I have found the Good Shepherd to be the calm peace that my heart, mind, and soul desired as He rejoiced over me with singing. I too have felt the raging seas of storms and trials as their waves sought to toss me to and fro. I have felt the draining dehydration of the trials as they seemed to zap all strength from my body. In those moments the Good Shepherd who says to the waves and the storm, "Peace, be still" has stilled every quaking wave in my heart and mind.

The comparisons could go on and on, and the declaration would still be the same. The Lord is my Shepherd. I have all that I need. Let's take a few minutes today and praise this Good Shepherd who has led us in every good path, who has provided all we need, and has restored all that we have ever lost on our own.

*"Evening and morning and at noon I will pray, and cry aloud,
and He shall hear my voice."*
Psalm 55:17

Magnify!
The Good Shepherd

"A Psalm. Give ear, O Shepherd of Israel, You who lead Joseph like a flock; You who dwell between the cherubim, shine forth!"
Psalm 80:1

"You are my flock, the sheep of my pasture. You are my people, and I am your God. I, the Sovereign LORD, have spoken!"
Ezekiel 34:31 (NLT)

"I am the Good Shepherd. The good shepherd lays down his life for the sheep. The hired hand is not the shepherd and does not own the sheep. So when he sees the wolf coming, he abandons the sheep and runs away. Then the wolf attacks the flock and scatters it. The man runs away because he is a hired hand and cares nothing for the sheep. I am the good shepherd; I know my sheep and my sheep know me— just as the Father knows me and I know the Father—and I lay down my life for the sheep. I have other sheep that are not of this sheep pen. I must bring them also. They too will listen to my voice, and there shall be one flock and one shepherd."
John 10:11-16 (NIV)

"He will feed his flock like a shepherd. He will carry the lambs in his arms, holding them close to his heart.
He will gently lead the mother sheep with their young."
Isaiah 40:11 (NLT)

"Save your people and bless your inheritance;
be their shepherd and carry them forever."
Psalm 28:9 (NIV)

"the God who has been my shepherd all my life long to this day"
Genesis 48:15 (ESV)

"Now the tax collectors and sinners were all drawing near to hear him. And the Pharisees and the scribes grumbled, saying, 'This man receives sinners and eats with them.' So he told them this parable: 'What man of you, having a hundred sheep, if he has lost one of them, does not leave the ninety-nine in the open country, and go after the one that is lost, until he finds it? And when he has found it, he lays it on his shoulders, rejoicing. And when he comes home, he calls together his friends and his neighbors, saying to them, 'Rejoice with me, for I have found my sheep that was lost.' Just so, I tell you, there will be more joy in heaven over one sinner who repents than over ninety-nine righteous persons who need no repentance.'"
Luke 15:1-7 (ESV)

"For thus says the Lord GOD: "Indeed I Myself will search for My sheep and seek them out. As a shepherd seeks out his flock on the day he is among his scattered sheep, so will I seek out My sheep and deliver them from all the places where they were scattered on a cloudy and dark day. And I will bring them out from the peoples and gather them from the countries, and will bring them to their own land; I will feed them on the mountains of Israel, in the valleys and in all the inhabited places of the country. I will feed them in good pasture, and their fold shall be on the high mountains of Israel. There they shall lie down in a good fold and feed in rich pasture on the mountains of Israel. I will feed My flock, and I will make them lie down,' says the Lord GOD. 'I will seek what was lost and bring back what was driven away,
bind up the broken and strengthen what was sick'"
Ezekiel 34:11-16

"'And you, O Bethlehem, in the land of Judah,
are by no means least among the rulers of Judah;
for from you shall come a ruler
who will shepherd my people Israel.'"
Matthew 2:6 (ESV)

"Listen to this message from the LORD, you nations of the world; proclaim it in distant coastlands: The LORD, who scattered his people, will gather them and watch over them as a shepherd does his flock."
Jeremiah 31:10 (NLT)

> "Enter into His gates with thanksgiving, and into His courts with praise. Be thankful to Him, and bless His name. For the LORD is good; His mercy is everlasting, and His truth endures to all generations."
> Psalm 100:4-5

Thank You Jesus today for…

_____
_____
_____
_____
_____
_____
_____
_____
_____
_____
_____
_____
_____
_____
_____
_____
_____
_____
_____
_____
_____
_____
_____
_____
_____
_____
_____
_____
_____
_____

Day 15
Magnify!
God our Rock

When I was in Ninth grade, our church's youth group took a missions trip up to northern California where we spent our time street witnessing and doing special evangelical events at the different churches that we were visiting. Our youth pastor wanted to end the trip with a few days of fun reward for all of our hard work, so he took us hiking up in the Sierra Nevadas and white-water river rafting down the American River. For three nights we camped on top of massive granite rock ledges that loomed over the valley. I remember feeling such safety as we slept above the rest of the earth with our sleeping bags laid out on top of some of the biggest granite rocks I'd ever seen! Yet in all of the solidity and massiveness of the Sierra Nevada granite cliffs, they still can't come anywhere close to being as firm, safe, solid, reliable, or massive as our God is.

> "Hear my cry, O God; Attend to my prayer.
> From the end of the earth I will cry to You,
> when my heart is overwhelmed;
> Lead me to the rock that is higher than I."
> Psalm 61.1-2

Maybe David was seeking safety as high up in the cliffs of Israel as he could physically be when he realized within his soul that he needed to be taken up even higher than the earth could offer. David wanted to be higher than the fear and worry that were overwhelming his heart, and higher up than his enemy's ability to climb and hunt. I'm sure we've all felt those moments of helplessness that come from the panicked feeling of life closing in upon us. David knew that only God could lift him high above the chaos of circumstances that he was facing. Sometimes life floods us with troubles and its circumstances seem to be intentionally directed toward shaking us. And yet, in every storm, through every season, and within every trial, we have the rock of Christ. When life overwhelms us, God leads us to the ground that is higher than the flood, steadier than the shaking ground, firmer than the sinking mud, and more solid than even the most tangible areas of life. The Rock of Christ provides all that we need in every moment of life.

I love that God likens Himself to our rock. It's really interesting when you think about all we can do in life with rocks! We climb rocks to gain a better perspective of our surroundings. We take cover beneath them during storms. We hide behind them to have shelter from the enemy. We use them as stable high ground during earthquakes and floods. We use them as territory markers to guide our way… the list could go on and on! And then you think about those uses in light of God declaring Himself to be our Rock- it's amazing! Jesus is the Rock that gives us a heavenly perspective as He enables us to walk on the high hills above the chaos, drama, floundering and flooding of this world. Jesus is the Rock that shelters us from the storms of life as He becomes our strong tower and fortress from the winds and rains. Jesus is the Rock that becomes our hiding place from the enemy as He covers us with His hand and protects us through the strength of His name. Jesus is the rock that provides a stable and firm ground for us to stand upon so that we can be His people who will not be moved and will never be shaken. Jesus is the Rock that leads us and guides us along the paths that He has ordained for us as we follow hard after Him. With all of this and more, no wonder Moses declares in Deuteronomy 32 that the rock of the world is not like our Rock!

Our family loves to camp in Yosemite, and my son has spent years scaling every rock we walk by to see how high up he could get and how far he could go, jumping from rock to rock. One thing that I love about hiking in Yosemite is that there are always rocks that are big enough to challenge my son's climbing ability, no matter how much bigger he grows! When the Israelites were dehydrated in the wilderness they cried out in complaint toward Moses, who in turn cried out to God, knowing that He alone could quench the thirst of His people. God worked a miracle, twice bringing water from the rock to satiate the thirst of His people. 1 Corinthians gives us insight that they drank from the same rock that we do, and that spiritual Rock is Christ. Jesus, our Rock, satisfies our thirst in the difficult places, brings satiation in the places of drought, and water to the parched dry desert-scape areas of our lives. Like my son who will never "outgrow" the massive rocks in Yosemite, you and I will never find our needs to be greater than the miracles that the Lord our Rock can provide. He will always be bigger, stronger, mightier, and much more massive than anything that comes our way in this world today. We are the people who stand surefooted, not because of the strength within our own feet, but because of the strength of the God that we stand upon! The rocks of this world won't ever be able to compare the massive Rock of our God!

"Evening and morning and at noon I will pray, and cry aloud, and He shall hear my voice."
Psalm 55:17

Magnify!
God our Rock

"All of them ate the same spiritual food, and all of them drank the same spiritual water. For they drank from the spiritual rock that traveled with them, and that rock was Christ."
1 Corinthians 10:3-4 (NLT)

"He alone is my rock and my salvation, my fortress where I will never be shaken."
Psalm 62:2 (NLT)

"You are coming to Christ, who is the living cornerstone of God's temple. He was rejected by people, but he was chosen by God for great honor. And you are living stones that God is building into his spiritual temple. What's more, you are his holy priests. Through the mediation of Jesus Christ, you offer spiritual sacrifices that please God. As the Scriptures say, 'I am placing a cornerstone in Jerusalem, chosen for great honor, and anyone who trusts in him will never be disgraced.' Yes, you who trust him recognize the honor God has given him. But for those who reject him, 'The stone that the builders rejected has now become the cornerstone.' And, 'He is the stone that makes people stumble, the rock that makes them fall.' They stumble because they do not obey God's word, and so they meet the fate that was planned for them."
1 Peter 2:4-8 (NLT)

"My heart rejoices in the LORD! The LORD has made me strong. Now I have an answer for my enemies; I rejoice because you rescued me. No one is holy like the LORD! There is no one besides you; there is no Rock like our God."
1 Samuel 2:1-2 (NLT)

"I will proclaim the name of the LORD; how glorious is our God! He is the Rock; his deeds are perfect. Everything he does is just and fair. He is a faithful God who does no wrong; how just and upright he is!"
Deuteronomy 32:3-4 (NLT)

"When Jesus came into the region of Caesarea Philippi, He asked His disciples, saying, "Who do men say that I, the Son of Man, am?" So they said, "Some say John the Baptist, some Elijah, and others Jeremiah or one of the prophets." He said to them, "But who do you say that I am?" Simon Peter answered and said, "You are the Christ, the Son of the living God." Jesus answered and said to him, "Blessed are you, Simon Bar-Jonah, for flesh and blood has not revealed this to you, but My Father who is in heaven. And I also say to you that you are Peter, and on this rock I will build My church, and the gates of Hades shall not prevail against it. 19 And I will give you the keys of the kingdom of heaven, and whatever you bind on earth will be bound in heaven, and whatever you loose on earth will be loosed in heaven."
Matthew 16:13-19

"You neglected the Rock who had fathered you; you forgot the God who had given you birth."
Deuteronomy 32:18 (NLT)

"To You I will cry, O LORD my Rock: Do not be silent to me, Lest, if You are silent to me, I become like those who go down to the pit."
Psalm 28:1

"Listen to me, you who pursue righteousness, you who seek the LORD: look to the rock from which you were hewn, and to the quarry from which you were dug."
Isaiah 51:1 (ESV)

"I love you, LORD; You are my strength. The LORD is my rock, my fortress, and my savior; my God is my rock, in whom I find protection. He is my shield, the power that saves me, and my place of safety. I called on the LORD, who is worthy of praise, and he saved me from my enemies… For who is God except the LORD? Who but our God is a solid rock?... The LORD lives! Praise to my Rock! May the God of my salvation be exalted!"
Psalm 18:1-3, 31, 46 (NLT)

"Enter into His gates with thanksgiving, and into His courts with praise. Be thankful to Him, and bless His name. For the LORD is good; His mercy is everlasting, and His truth endures to all generations."
Psalm 100:4-5

Thank You Jesus today for…

Day 16
Magnify!
Forgiveness

If you're like me, there's countless times a day that you mess up, say something you shouldn't, do something you knew better than, or just plain blow it. Is there any greater feeling than when those we've affected in our mistakes, mess-ups, and meltdowns choose to forgive us? What sweetness we feel when the victims of our carelessness have chosen to understand our intents or lapses of sound judgments and continue on with the relationship in spite of our failings. It feels wonderful when we are forgiven by equally sinful humans, but how much more so when we're talking about the God who has the only justified perfect standard in existence! There was a time in Luke where the feet of Jesus were being kissed and cried upon with the oil, lips, and tears of a sinful woman who had been greatly forgiven by God. Some in the room were appalled that Jesus would let such a woman near Him, and yet I love the gracious, forgiving, merciful response of Jesus in this moment.

"And Jesus answering said to him, 'Simon, I have something to say to you.' And he answered, 'Say it, Teacher.' 'A certain moneylender had two debtors. One owed five hundred denarii, and the other fifty. When they could not pay, he cancelled the debt of both. Now which of them will love him more?' Simon answered, 'The one, I suppose, for whom he cancelled the larger debt.' And he said to him, 'You have judged rightly.' Then turning toward the woman he said to Simon, 'Do you see this woman? I entered your house; you gave me no water for my feet, but she has wet my feet with her tears and wiped them with her hair. You gave me no kiss, but from the time I came in she has not ceased to kiss my feet. You did not anoint my head with oil, but she has anointed my feet with ointment. Therefore I tell you, her sins, which are many, are forgiven—for she loved much. But he who is forgiven little, loves little.' And he said to her, 'Your sins are forgiven.' Then those who were at table with him began to say among themselves, 'Who is this, who even forgives sins?'"
Luke 7:40-49 (ESV)

You and I owed a debt that we could not pay. We owed the debt of our own miserable sin. We owed the debt of our inability to be who we desired to be. We owed the debt of our failed purity. We owed the debt of our pride and selfishness. And yet in light of all the ways I've failed, it astounds me that my heart can often be like Simon's here in this chapter.

I know how incredibly short I fall, and yet somehow my eyes can still become critical toward another. We're desperately thankful for the forgiveness of God that we have received, and yet somehow still feel qualified to determine the worth of another to receive the same gift.

Yet, here was this precious girl, not caring who was around, who was observing, or who was commenting on her actions. She was so consumed in thankfulness of all that she had been forgiven that she was focused on the God of that forgiveness alone. Sometimes walking closely with Jesus can give us the illusion in our minds that we really aren't being forgiven for much. Jesus isn't saying that we have to have lived the life of a wretched sinner in order to love Him much. It's also the ones who live with an awareness of who we would be without Him that love Him much. It's also the ones who live with an awareness of all that He has saved us from having to experience that love Him much. Even if you grew up loving God, or have loved Him for years, it only takes a moment's glance into our fleshly tendencies to cause us to fall on our knees, in awe of His love and forgiveness, and thank Him profusely for all of the times He graciously *kept us* from running into sin.

All have sinned and missed the mark, and that is exclusive of none. And yet Jesus, the glorious spotless Lamb, chose to trade lives with us. He knows our hands move toward sin and that our feet have the propensity to run to evil, so He let His spotless hands and feet be nailed to the tree so that we could have the forgiveness of His perfection. This God filled with infinite perfection chose to take on our infinite imperfections, and to fill them instead with unending forgiveness. With all of this cleansing and purifying how could we not also sob at the feet of Jesus for all He erased? His perfect love has looked at us with such gracious eyes!

In light of how much we have been forgiven, is there someone you need to extend God's forgiveness to today? Who are we to hold a standard of unforgiveness against another? Take a couple minutes to ask God to show you how to move past the reality of your human hurt and to bestow His gift of forgiveness upon them. Thinking about God's great love toward you, and how much He endured for the opportunity to forgive you, is there something you've been holding onto, either out of guilt, shame, or a continued desire? Spend a few minutes releasing your hold upon this world and let Him wash your heart with forgiveness, purity, and newness.

*"Evening and morning and at noon I will pray, and cry aloud,
and He shall hear my voice."*
Psalm 55:17

Magnify!
Forgiveness

"Therefore, as God's chosen people, holy and dearly loved, clothe yourselves with compassion, kindness, humility, gentleness and patience. Bear with each other and forgive one another if any of you has a grievance against someone. Forgive as the Lord forgave you. And over all these virtues put on love, which binds them
all together in perfect unity."
Colossians 3:12-14 (NIV)

"I, even I, am he who blots out
your transgressions, for my own sake,
and remembers your sins no more."
Isaiah 43:25 (NIV)

"And forgive us our debts, as we also have forgiven our debtors.
And lead us not into temptation, but deliver us from the evil one.
For if you forgive other people when they sin against you, your heavenly Father will also forgive you. But if you do not forgive others their sins, your Father will not forgive your sins."
Matthew 6:12-14 (ESV)

"So watch yourselves. If your brother or sister sins against you, rebuke them; and if they repent, forgive them. Even if they sin against you seven times in a day and seven times come back to you saying
'I repent,' you must forgive them.
The apostles said to the Lord, 'Increase our faith!'"
Luke 17:3-5 (NIV)

"Repent, then, and turn to God, so that your sins may be wiped out, that times of refreshing may come from the Lord"
Acts 3:19 (NIV)

"If we say that we have no sin, we deceive ourselves, and the truth is not in us. If we confess our sins, He is faithful and just to forgive us our sins and to cleanse us from all unrighteousness."
1 John 1:8-9

"The Lord our God is merciful and forgiving, even though we have rebelled against him"
Daniel 9:9 (NIV)

"And do not grieve the Holy Spirit of God, with whom you were sealed for the day of redemption. Get rid of all bitterness, rage and anger, brawling and slander, along with every form of malice. Be kind and compassionate to one another, forgiving each other, just as in Christ God forgave you."
Ephesians 4:30-32 (NIV)

"'Come now, let us settle the matter,' says the LORD. 'Though your sins are like scarlet, they shall be as white as snow; though they are red as crimson, they shall be like wool.'"
Isaiah 1:18 (NIV)

"Therefore, if anyone is in Christ, the new creation has come: The old has gone, the new is here! All this is from God, who reconciled us to himself through Christ and gave us the ministry of reconciliation: that God was reconciling the world to Himself in Christ, not counting people's sins against them. And he has committed to us the message of reconciliation. We are therefore Christ's ambassadors, as though God were making his appeal through us. We implore you on Christ's behalf: Be reconciled to God. God made him who had no sin to be sin for us, so that in him we might become the righteousness of God."
2 Corinthians 5:17-21 (NIV)

"For as high as the heavens are above the earth, so great is his love for those who fear him; as far as the east is from the west, so far has he removed our transgressions from us."
Psalm 103:11-12 (NIV)

"Enter into His gates with thanksgiving, and into His courts with praise. Be thankful to Him, and bless His name. For the LORD is good; His mercy is everlasting, and His truth endures to all generations."
Psalm 100:4-5

Thank You Jesus today for…

_____
_____
_____
_____
_____
_____
_____
_____
_____
_____
_____
_____
_____
_____
_____
_____
_____
_____
_____
_____
_____
_____
_____
_____
_____
_____
_____
_____

Day 17
Magnify!
His Help

Chased by enemies. Hunted down like a wild animal. Innocent, yet wrongly accused. Was there ever a recorded Biblical character who needed more help than David? We find verse after verse in the book of Psalms, written with desperate cries for help and answered by God, the Ever-Present Help in time of need. The revelations of God as our helper belong to those who are often in desperate need of help. When we look to God we are saved, because He is our help. When we look to God we are satisfied, because He is our help. When we look to God we are filled with faith, because He is our help.

"But you, O LORD, do not be far off! O you my help,
come quickly to my aid!"
Psalm 22:19 (ESV)
"The LORD is my strength and my shield; in him my heart trusts, and I am helped; my heart exults, and with my song I give thanks to him."
Psalm 28:7 (ESV)
"Hear, O LORD, and be merciful to me! O LORD, be my helper!"
Psalm 30:10 (ESV)
"Our soul waits for the LORD; he is our help and our shield."
Psalm 33:20 (ESV)
"Behold, God is my helper; the Lord is the upholder of my life."
Psalm 54:4 (ESV)
"Our help is in the name of the LORD, who made heaven and earth."
Psalm 124:8 (ESV)

On and on throughout the book of Psalms come the cries for help and the answers from heaven. On and on throughout the book of Psalms come the declarations of weakness in humanity and the promised help from God through the strength of His infinite power. We are the people who are never left nor forsaken. We are the people who are promised the ability to walk without growing weary, and to run without growing faint. Jesus is ever present, always ready to save, always watching, always able, and always more than enough. There is no victory that cannot be won through the help of our God. There is no relationship that cannot be salvaged through the help of our God. There is no person that cannot be redeemed through the help of our God. There is no anger that cannot be cooled through the help of our God. There is no desperation that cannot be answered through the help of our God. Nothing is too far gone or too far away. Nothing is out of His reach.

Nothing is too difficult to accomplish with the help of our God. Nothing is impossible for our God! All can be helped. All can be redeemed. All can be restored. Those who regularly cry out to God for help will find Him more than able, more than adequate, more than enough, and more than sufficient. Our cry for help is not answered by One who is limited in His abilities. Our cry for help is answered by the mighty God who declares that His arm is not so short that He cannot save.

That being said, we also know that God's help doesn't always come in the form of what we expected our help to look like. God's help doesn't come in the form of wishes granted by a genie in the sky, or a pain-free life of ease. I remember learning as a little girl that helping a butterfly emerge from its cocoon would actually bring about its death. It felt almost impossible to just sit beside it and watch the process without intervening! The butterfly's struggle was part of the strengthening process, and there was no greater help that could be offered than to let it struggle in order to release its wings. The struggle would enable the butterfly to strengthen its wings and fly. This reminds me of the type of help we read about in Mark 9. A father, desperate for his son's healing brings his demon possessed child to Jesus for healing. Jesus declares that anything is possible for the ones who believe, and the father's answer is one that encourages my heart every time I read it. Immediately the father of the child cried out and said, "I believe; help my unbelief!" Often God's help comes in the form of a wall, an impossibility, a tragedy, a disbelief, or a difficulty. God brings us to the place where we can no longer rely on our own ingenuity or ability. The circumstances are too impossible, and we're left with the struggle of our weakness, the struggle of our incapability, and the struggle of our inability to accomplish that which is needed. God's help doesn't always take away the pain, circumstances, or crisis. But His help always proves more than able to walk us out to the other side, stronger, more valiant, and able to fly higher than ever before.

God's ever-present help is the help that brings us strength in our weakness, faith in our fear, boldness in our timidity, and confidence in our insecurity. God doesn't promise that there will be no fire, floods, or trials to walk through. But He does promise that He will walk these strengthening moments with us in order to bring beauty from the ashes, praise from the weakness, and joy from the mourning. I'm ever grateful that the help of God is only a cry away, and often comes before I'm even aware to cry out. His help strengthens us, sustains us, satisfies us, and speaks life to us. The ever-present help of God is like none other!

"Evening and morning and at noon I will pray, and cry aloud, and He shall hear my voice."
Psalm 55:17

Magnify!
His Help

"Don't be afraid, for I am with you. Don't be discouraged, for I am your God. I will strengthen you and help you. I will hold you up with my victorious right hand."
Isaiah 41:10 (NLT)

"For God has said, 'I will never fail you. I will never abandon you.' So we can say with confidence, 'The LORD is my Helper, so I will have no fear. What can mere people do to me?'"
Hebrews 13:5-6 (NLT)

"I look up to the mountains— does my help come from there? My help comes from the LORD, who made heaven and earth!"
Psalm 121:1-2 (NLT)

"This High Priest of ours understands our weaknesses, for he faced all of the same testings we do, yet he did not sin. So let us come boldly to the throne of our gracious God. There we will receive his mercy, and we will find grace to help us when we need it most."
Hebrews 4:15-16 (NLT)

"The LORD is for me, so I will have no fear. What can mere people do to me? Yes, the LORD is for me; he will help me. I will look in triumph at those who hate me. It is better to take refuge in the LORD than to trust in people. It is better to take refuge in the LORD than to trust in princes."
Psalm 118:6-9 (NLT)

"But the Helper, the Holy Spirit, whom the Father will send in My name, He will teach you all things, and bring to your remembrance all things that I said to you"
John 14:26

"God is our refuge and strength, a very present help in trouble. Therefore we will not fear though the earth gives way, though the mountains be moved into the heart of the sea, though its waters roar and foam, though the mountains tremble at its swelling. *Selah* There is a river whose streams make glad the city of God, the holy habitation of the Most High. God is in the midst of her; she shall not be moved; God will help her when morning dawns. The nations rage, the kingdoms totter; He utters his voice, the earth melts. The LORD of hosts is with us; the God of Jacob is our fortress. *Selah*"
Psalm 46:1-7

"See, all your angry enemies lie there, confused and humiliated. Anyone who opposes you will die and come to nothing. You will look in vain for those who tried to conquer you. Those who attack you will come to nothing. For I hold you by your right hand— I, the LORD your God. And I say to you, 'Don't be afraid. I am here to help you. Though you are a lowly worm, O Jacob, don't be afraid, people of Israel, for I will help you. I am the LORD, your Redeemer. I am the Holy One of Israel.'"
Isaiah 41:11-14 (NLT)

"There is no one like the God of Israel. He rides across the heavens to help you, across the skies in majestic splendor. The eternal God is your refuge, and his everlasting arms are under you."
Deuteronomy 33:26-27 (NLT)

"But when the Helper comes, whom I will send to you from the Father, the Spirit of truth, who proceeds from the Father, he will bear witness about me. And you also will bear witness, because you have been with me from the beginning."
John 15:26-27 (ESV)

"Our soul waits for the LORD; He is our help and our shield."
Psalm 33:20

"O LORD, no one but you can help the powerless against the mighty! Help us, O LORD our God, for we trust in you alone. It is in your name that we have come against this vast horde. O LORD, you are our God; do not let mere men prevail against you!"
2 Chronicles 14:11 (NLT)

> "Enter into His gates with thanksgiving, and into His courts with praise. Be thankful to Him, and bless His name.
> For the LORD is good; His mercy is everlasting, and His truth endures to all generations."
> Psalm 100:4-5

Thank You Jesus today for…

Day 18
Magnify!
God as our Husband

Have you ever sat down to talk with an engaged couple who's about to be married? If you can actually get them to stop gazing into each other's eyes and acknowledge you for a moment, you'll usually find that they truly think they'll be able to meet each other's deepest needs forever. Whether you're married or not, I think we all have a deep-down innate desire to be loved, wanted, cared for, provided for, and made happy by another. Problems arise in so many marriages when these desires are expected to be fulfilled by an earthly spouse. I have the greatest earthly husband that God ever formed, and yet in his humanity he still can't meet every need that I have, and I'm not even a very needy person! There is only one Husband who can meet every need, truly fill, completely satisfy, and forever satiate us. And that's our Maker, our Husband.

> "Do not be afraid; you will not be put to shame.
> Do not fear disgrace; you will not be humiliated.
> You will forget the shame of your youth
> and remember no more the reproach of your widowhood.
> For your Maker is your husband—
> the LORD Almighty is His name—
> the Holy One of Israel is your Redeemer;
> He is called the God of all the earth."
> Isaiah 54:4-59 (NIV)

Israel was having a problem, in that they forgot that God was the only one who would ever be able to fully satisfy them and love them in the way they desired. In their forgetfulness, they began to chase after other gods, which left them finding only emptiness and sorrow. Every need and desire we have can somewhat be filled with a great earthly relationship, but the substance of that fulfilled desire can be found in Christ alone. Jesus is the only One who can redeem us and give us the life, love, and identity we truly long to have. He's the only One who can grasp our deepest feelings and longings. A husband can look at a bride with such love, that for a season butterflies might flutter around within her, but eventually that continual infatuation fades into the routine of real life. The look of love from an earthly spouse wasn't meant to satisfy our longing hearts forever. Earthly love lasts by choice and can still burn bright for years upon years when fed with the right decisions and priorities, but it's the love of God that was meant to give our souls the butterflies of emotion for all of our days. It's God's love that lasts eternally. It's God's love that looks at us constantly with that special gaze, regardless of how wild we might look or behave. Earthly relationships can have their moments of giving and receiving beautiful gifts of love, but they're nothing like the gifts of love from our beautiful God. Each new day, regardless of the failings from the day before, our Maker, our Husband gifts us with new mercies, fresh grace, and His steadfast love that reaches to the sky.

Our title as the bride of Christ is what was meant to satisfy our deepest longing to be by another's side in full satisfaction forever. Earthy marriages and relationships can be beautiful pictures of God's love upon us, but they can never truly satisfy us as completely as God's love is able to. We are the brides of Christ! One day the trumpet will sound, and we'll be whisked away to our wedding at the marriage supper of the Lamb. Our fulfillment, contentment, satisfaction, and identity are not found in this life, on this earth, or within earthly relationships. This world can bless us. Our relationships can bring us joy. But in every joy filled moment there is a twinge within us desiring more, and that more is found in our Heavenly Husband alone. What freedom we have in our earthly relationships when there is no pressure to be satisfied from a human who was never designed to deliver all we desire.

Jonathan Edwards wrote a beautiful description of his beloved fiancé, Sarah, that always leaves me longing to know Jesus, my Husband, in a deeper way, and to love Him with a greater love. "They say there is a young lady in [New Haven] who is loved of that Great Being, who made and rules the world, and that there are certain seasons in which this Great Being, in some way or other invisible, comes to her and fills her mind with exceeding sweet delight; and that she hardly cares for anything, except to meditate on Him… She will sometimes go about from place to place, singing sweetly; and seems to be always full of joy and pleasure. She loves to be alone, walking in the fields and groves, and seems to have Someone invisible always conversing with her."

I pray that as we live out our earthly days, we will walk daily with our true Husband in joy, fulfillment, and full satisfaction. Even in the most beautiful of earthly loves, we will never find a love like His. Our Maker, our Husband longs to fill us with such sweet joy in His Presence and such sweet satisfaction from His love. May He be our First Love forever, because there is not another love we could ever find in this life like the love that our Maker, our Husband pours out upon us.

"Evening and morning and at noon I will pray, and cry aloud, and He shall hear my voice."
Psalm 55:17

Magnify!
God as our Husband

"I will make you my wife forever, showing you righteousness and justice, unfailing love and compassion.
I will be faithful to you and make you mine, and you will finally know me as the LORD."
Hosea 2:19-20 (NLT)

"Then I heard again what sounded like the shout of a vast crowd or the roar of mighty ocean waves or the crash of loud thunder: 'Praise the LORD! For the Lord our God, the Almighty, reigns. Let us be glad and rejoice, and let us give honor to him. For the time has come for the wedding feast of the Lamb, and his bride has prepared herself. She has been given the finest of pure white linen to wear.' For the fine linen represents the good deeds of God's holy people. And the angel said to me, 'Write this: Blessed are those who are invited to the wedding feast of the Lamb.' And he added, 'These are true words that come from God.'"
Revelation 19:6-9 (NLT)

"But then I will win her back once again.
I will lead her into the desert and speak tenderly to her there.
I will return her vineyards to her
and transform the Valley of Trouble into a gateway of hope.
She will give herself to me there,
as she did long ago when she was young,
when I freed her from her captivity in Egypt.
'When that day comes,' says the LORD,
'you will call me 'my husband'
instead of 'my master.'"
Hosea 2:14-16 (NLT)

"The LORD will hold you in His hand for all to see—
a splendid crown in the hand of God.
Never again will you be called "The Forsaken City"
or "The Desolate Land."
Your new name will be "The City of God's Delight"
and "The Bride of God," for the LORD delights in you
and will claim you as his bride.
Your children will commit themselves to you, O Jerusalem,
just as a young man commits himself to his bride.
Then God will rejoice over you
as a bridegroom rejoices over his bride."
Isaiah 62:3-5 (NLT)

"This is what the LORD says: "I remember how eager you were to please me as a young bride long ago, how you loved me and followed me even through the barren wilderness."
Jeremiah 2:2 (NLT)

"For I am jealous for you with the jealousy of God himself. I promised you as a pure bride to one husband—Christ. But I fear that somehow your pure and undivided devotion to Christ will be corrupted, just as Eve was deceived by the cunning ways of the serpent."
2 Corinthians 11:2-3 (NLT)

"So I wrapped my cloak around you to cover your nakedness and declared my marriage vows. I made a covenant with you, says the Sovereign LORD, and you became mine. "Then I bathed you and washed off your blood, and I rubbed fragrant oils into your skin. I gave you expensive clothing of fine linen and silk, beautifully embroidered, and sandals made of fine goatskin leather. I gave you lovely jewelry, bracelets, beautiful necklaces, a ring for your nose, earrings for your ears, and a lovely crown for your head. And so you were adorned with gold and silver. Your clothes were made of fine linen and costly fabric and were beautifully embroidered. You ate the finest foods—choice flour, honey, and olive oil—and became more beautiful than ever. You looked like a queen, and so you were! Your fame soon spread throughout the world because of your beauty. I dressed you in my splendor and perfected your beauty, says the Sovereign LORD."
Ezekiel 16:8-14 (NLT)

> "Enter into His gates with thanksgiving, and into His courts with praise. Be thankful to Him, and bless His name. For the LORD is good; His mercy is everlasting, and His truth endures to all generations."
> Psalm 100:4-5

Thank You Jesus today for…

_____
_____
_____
_____
_____
_____
_____
_____
_____
_____
_____
_____
_____
_____
_____
_____
_____
_____
_____
_____
_____
_____
_____
_____
_____
_____
_____

Day 19
Magnify!
Mercy

I'm sure we've all seen the movies or read the stories where someone is about to feel the full consequences of their actions and cries out, "Mercy! Mercy!" Meaning what? "Go easy on me!" "Don't punish me to the full extent of what I deserve!" When a heart truly understands the extent of the eternal death we face as the consequences for our sins, we cry out for mercy as well. The righteous standard of God is one of perfect Holiness, and we fall incredibly short. The wages of sin is death, and God, being a just Judge, has to issue out the right sentence. And we understand this in our world. Let's say you witnessed a murder or a crime against someone you loved. As the day for the trial came, all the evidence was there mounting against them; that person was guilty of hurting someone dear to your heart. But what if the criminal walked into the courtroom and cried out for mercy to be given to them instead of the consequences of their actions? And what if the judge said, "You know what, I'm a nice person and you really want mercy, so I'm going to go ahead and let you off." Would you feel like justice had been done? God is a just Judge and He would be less than just if He showered the guilty with mercy simply because they desired it. While it's true that God is absolute justice, He is also absolute love. He knew that the cost of our sin was too great for us to pay. Desiring us to live in full access of His Presence, He took up His own righteous standard of holiness and came to earth to live a perfect life. Jesus traded lives with us so that our sin could be atoned for and so that mercy could be bought.

> "And you shall put the mercy seat on the top of the ark, and in the ark you shall put the testimony that I shall give you. There I will meet with you and from above the mercy seat, from between the cherubim that are on the ark of the testimony, I will speak with you about all that I will give you in our commandment for the people of Israel... and the veil shall separate for you the Holy Place from the Most Holy. You shall put the mercy seat on the ark of the testimony in the Most Holy Place"
> Exodus 25:21-22, 26:33-34 (ESV)

We were separated from full-flowing mercy by the veil of God's perfect Holiness until our beautiful Savior became our perfect sacrifice upon the cross. Thanks be to God who has made a way and torn the veil so that we could run into His Presence and obtain mercy in time of need! Until this moment, the most needed place was the most untouchable place. We see in Leviticus that it was quite a process for even the high priest to come into the holy of holies before the mercy seat. There were specific clothes that needed to be worn as a covering. There were specific animals that were needed as an offering. There was specific bathing that needed to be done as a cleansing. There was specific incense needed to be burnt as a covering… all of this so that the high priest "does not die" as he enters the area of the mercy seat. But then our great High Priest came to tear the veil and open up the Presence of the LORD because at last the perfect life was lived by our God who chose to take up our humanity and live the perfect life for us. The veil has been torn and we are granted access in freedom because of the sacrifice of Jesus upon the cross. How wonderful that we no longer have to fear death as we run into the Presence of God to obtain the mercy we so desperately need and desire. We are no longer stained by our sin, we are covered with the cloud of His Presence and washed clean by His cleansing blood. We have all the mercy we desire in spite of our lack of holiness, because of the great holiness of the spotless Lamb upon us!

Until the cross of Christ, only one man once a year was allowed near the mercy seat to atone for the sins of the people. Until Jesus. Until the beautiful, spotless Lamb of God who could take away the sins of the earth came to that cross and declared us clean forever. "IT IS FINISHED!" He cried out as the atoning for the sins of the world was completed, paving the way for all who wanted mercy to run to Him. Jesus bore our sins so that we could be cleansed and forever washed clean by the blood of the Lamb. Forever we were set free by the grace of God. Forever our lives are covered by the blood of the Spotless Lamb. Forever we are able to run into His throne room to obtain mercy in time of need. We were purchased at a price and that cost was the life of Jesus. Because of that you and I can cry out for mercy, and God, the Just Judge, can rightly pour out goodness upon a life that deserves only pain, punishment, death and separation. We can run to the mercy seat that we could never approach before. We can obtain the very breath of purity that we never had access to. We can breathe in the very presence of the holiness of God because the spotless Lamb has taken away our sins and has chosen to set us free.

Thank You Jesus for providing us with the way to You! Oh, that we would always have a mercy seat within our souls as a place set aside for God to meet with us, speak to us, and shower us with all of the cleansing mercy that we need. We can draw near in boldness and absolute confidence, not because of any good within us, but because of the faithful, precious goodness of Jesus who opened the way into His presence and abundantly filled our life with His mercy!

"Evening and morning and at noon I will pray, and cry aloud, and He shall hear my voice."
Psalm 55:17

Magnify!
Mercy

"For we do not have a high priest who is unable to empathize with our weaknesses, but we have one who has been tempted in every way, just as we are—yet he did not sin. Let us then approach God's throne of grace with confidence, so that we may receive mercy and find grace to help us in our time of need."
Hebrews 4:15-16 (NIV)

"Who is a God like you, who pardons sin and forgives the transgression of the remnant of his inheritance? You do not stay angry forever but delight to show mercy.
You will again have compassion on us"
Micah 7:18-19 (NIV)

"But go and learn what this means: 'I desire mercy, not sacrifice.' For I did not come to call the righteous, but sinners, to repentance."
Matthew 9:13

"Have mercy on me, O God, according to your unfailing love; according to your great compassion blot out my transgressions. Wash away all my iniquity and cleanse me from my sin."
Psalm 51:1-2 (NIV)

"All of us also lived among them at one time, gratifying the cravings of our flesh and following its desires and thoughts. Like the rest, we were by nature deserving of wrath. But because of his great love for us, God, who is rich in mercy, made us alive with Christ even when we were dead in transgressions—it is by grace you have been saved."
Ephesians 2:3-5 (NIV)

"Surely goodness and mercy shall follow me All the days of my life; And I will dwell in the house of the LORD Forever."
Psalm 23:6

"for the LORD your God is gracious and merciful, and will not turn His face from you if you return to Him."
2 Chronicles 30:9

"Do not withhold Your tender mercies from me, O LORD; Let Your lovingkindness and Your truth continually preserve me."
Psalm 40:11

"Therefore the LORD will wait, that He may be gracious to you; And therefore He will be exalted, that He may have mercy on you. For the LORD is a God of justice; Blessed are all those who wait for Him."
Isaiah 30:18

"Remember, LORD, your great mercy and love, for they are from of old. Do not remember the sins of my youth and my rebellious ways; according to your love remember me, for you, LORD, are good."
Psalm 25:6-7 (NIV)

"Therefore, I urge you, brothers and sisters, in view of God's mercy, to offer your bodies as a living sacrifice, holy and pleasing to God— this is your true and proper worship."
Romans 12:1 (NIV)

"But in your great mercy, you did not destroy them completely or abandon them forever. What a gracious and merciful God you are!"
Nehemiah 9:31 (NLT)

"Go, and proclaim these words toward the north, and say, "Return, faithless Israel, declares the LORD. I will not look on you in anger, for I am merciful, declares the LORD; I will not be angry forever."
Jeremiah 3:12 (ESV)

"Let the wicked change their ways and banish the very thought of doing wrong. Let them turn to the LORD that he may have mercy on them. Yes, turn to our God, for he will forgive generously."
Isaiah 55:7 (NLT)

"Enter into His gates with thanksgiving, and into His courts with praise. Be thankful to Him, and bless His name. For the LORD is good; His mercy is everlasting, and His truth endures to all generations."
Psalm 100:4-5

Thank You Jesus today for…

Day 20
Magnify!
Creator God

Imagine that you're making something; a meal, a blanket, a craft, a dress- absolutely anything at all. Now picture that whatever it is you're creating suddenly looks up at you and declares, "This isn't how you should do it! You should have done it this way!" As crazy as that would be to experience, we're still just finite humans and probably *are* doing it wrong! We adults know that we have a greater understanding of the workings of the world than small children and inanimate objects, but we still go about things in the wrong way. I'm sure there are much easier ways to accomplish most things that I do. But when you think about God's wisdom in comparison to ours, His ability in comparison to ours, and His Infinite mind in comparison to our extremely finite minds, suddenly we seem like the silly ones for ever questioning Him in anything that He chooses to do!

> "I create the light and make the darkness. I send good times and bad times. I, the LORD, am the one who does these things. Open up, O heavens, and pour out your righteousness. Let the earth open wide so salvation and righteousness can sprout up together.
> I, the LORD, created them. What sorrow awaits those who argue with their Creator. Does a clay pot argue with its maker? Does the clay dispute with the one who shapes it, saying, 'Stop, you're doing it wrong!' Does the pot exclaim, 'How clumsy can you be?' How terrible it would be if a newborn baby said to its father, 'Why was I born?' or if it said to its mother, 'Why did you make me this way?' This is what the LORD says— the Holy One of Israel and your Creator:
> Do you question what I do for my children? Do you give me orders about the work of my hands? I am the one who made the earth and created people to live on it. With my hands I stretched out the heavens. All the stars are at my command."
> Isaiah 45:7-12 (NLT)

We read these verses, and the concept of a clay pot arguing with its maker seem funny to us because we know that even if a little clay pot could speak, it still wouldn't know anywhere near as much as the one who was able to make it. Yet how many times I have been one of those little clay pots arguing with my Maker about how He has created me or how He is orchestrating my life. Many of us have dealt with a child throwing a temper tantrum over essential concepts of life that they are too young to understand. In love we hold our ground, knowing that our adamancy is protecting them from something they have yet to grasp. And yet how often I have been that child throwing the temper tantrum over something that the Heavenly Father seems to be withholding from me. Hindsight shows His wisdom, but the moment shows my flesh. Hindsight shows His greater understanding, but the moment shows my ignorance. Sorrow awaits the ones who argue, not because punishment is coming, but because peace is found in the life that obeys God and submits to the Creator's good hand. Our finite understanding cannot see the end of His plans, but His perfect vision surpasses time and space. He's the Alpha and the Omega; the Beginning and the End. He's the Author and the Finisher, and what He deems good and necessary is good and necessary whether we can see the good reasoning and sense or not. God's creation process is not like our creation process. We create in hope that what we're making will turn out and not become a created failure. But our Good Creator knows the way we take and beyond a shadow of a doubt will produce within us the exact creation that He desires.

It's not that I generally disagree with the statement that God is the good Creator of my life. It's just that I usually have an idea of what He's going to create, when He's going to create it, and how that creation process within me will take place. It honestly boils down to the fact that I have different plans for me. We tend to have our own plans of what we want our lives to look like and or our own ideas of the directions we'd like to go in. When those plans, ideas, and assumptions get interrupted we can be trapped into thinking things are falling apart, when actually, in light of the true plans of the good Creator, things are falling right into place. No one can know God's plans from beginning to end, but He unfolds His creation of our days in the exact way He has designed them to be.

Even as the creation process took place in Genesis, the Holy Spirit is now hovering over the face of our nothingness, ready to fill it with His holy goodness in the way that He sees fit. He creates light where there has been only darkness. He creates beauty where there have been only ashes. He creates purpose where there has been only floundering. He creates life where there has been only death. He allows the bad things as well as the good, but only so that He can work it for good within our lives, or so that He can produce good within us. We might not be able to see His plans, ideas, and reasonings, but we can trust that the good hand of our holy Creator is always creating that which we will eventually declare to be good.

"Evening and morning and at noon I will pray, and cry aloud, and He shall hear my voice."
Psalm 55:17

Magnify!
Creator God

"In the beginning God created the heavens and the earth."
Genesis 1:1

"By faith we understand that the universe was formed at God's command, so that what is seen was not made out of what was visible."
Hebrews 11:3 (NIV)

"God saw all that he had made, and it was very good."
Genesis 1:31 (NIV)

"The Son is the image of the invisible God, the firstborn over all creation. For in him all things were created: things in heaven and on earth, visible and invisible, whether thrones or powers or rulers or authorities; all things have been created through him and for him. He is before all things, and in him all things hold together. And he is the head of the body, the church; he is the beginning and the firstborn from among the dead, so that in everything
he might have the supremacy."
Colossians 1:15-18 (NIV)

"Before the mountains were born, before you gave birth to the earth and the world, from beginning to end, you are God."
Psalm 90:2 (NLT)

"In the beginning was the Word, and the Word was with God, and the Word was God. He was with God in the beginning. Through him all things were made; without him nothing was made that has been made. In him was life, and that life was the light of all mankind."
John 1:1-4 (NIV)

"The LORD wraps himself in light as with a garment; he stretches out the heavens like a tent and lays the beams of his upper chambers on their waters. he makes the clouds his chariot and rides on the wings of the wind. He makes winds his messengers, flames of fire his servants.
He set the earth on its foundations; it can never be moved.
You covered it with the watery depths as with a garment; the waters stood above the mountains. But at your rebuke the waters fled, at the sound of your thunder they took to flight; they flowed over the mountains, they went down into the valleys, to the place you assigned for them. You set a boundary they cannot cross; never again will they cover the earth. He makes springs pour water into the ravines; it flows between the mountains. They give water to all the beasts of the field; the wild donkeys quench their thirst. The birds of the sky nest by the waters; they sing among the branches. He waters the mountains from his upper chambers; the land is satisfied by the fruit of his work. He makes grass grow for the cattle, and plants for people to cultivate— bringing forth food from the earth: wine that gladdens human hearts, oil to make their faces shine, and bread that sustains their hearts. The trees of
the LORD are well watered, the cedars of Lebanon that he planted.
There the birds make their nests; the stork has its home in the junipers. The high mountains belong to the wild goats; the crags are a refuge for the hyrax. He made the moon to mark the seasons, and the sun knows when to go down. You bring darkness, it becomes night, and all the beasts of the forest prowl. The lions roar for their prey and seek their food from God. The sun rises, and they steal away; they return and lie down in their dens. Then people go out to their work, to their labor until evening. How many are your works, LORD! In wisdom you made them all; the earth is full of your creatures."
Psalm 104:2-24 (NIV)

"Blessed be your glorious name, and may it be exalted above all blessing and praise. You alone are the LORD. You made the heavens, even the highest heavens, and all their starry host, the earth and all that is on it, the seas and all that is in them. You give life to everything, and the multitudes of heaven worship you."
Nehemiah 9:5-6 (NIV)

"You are worthy, O Lord our God, to receive glory and honor and power. For you created all things, and they exist
because you created what you pleased."
Revelation 4:11 (NLT)

> "Enter into His gates with thanksgiving, and into His courts with praise. Be thankful to Him, and bless His name. For the LORD is good; His mercy is everlasting, and His truth endures to all generations."
> Psalm 100:4-5

Thank You Jesus today for…

_____
_____
_____
_____
_____
_____
_____
_____
_____
_____
_____
_____
_____
_____
_____
_____
_____
_____
_____
_____
_____
_____
_____
_____
_____
_____
_____
_____
_____

Day 21
Magnify!
God's Sovereignty

Once upon a time there was a wicked king who ruled his kingdom with a harsh selfishness that oppressed the people of his land. His absolute rule brought about terror and hardship, as he reigned only to bring his wicked heart pleasure. In another kingdom near that land, there was a sovereign king who ruled his people in grace, truth, and love. Though he had absolute reign and power, the people of the land found peace and rest in his sovereign reign, knowing that he was ever moving the kingdom in the direction for their good. While these sentences are the making of great fictional fairytales, they also shed light upon how we view the sovereignty of God. If the perspective and opinion of sovereignty varies, dependent upon the personality of the sovereign human, how much more so when we're dealing with the ultimate sovereignty of God! Those who fear and dislike the sovereignty of God do so only because they don't know the true character of the God who is only good continually. We have the High King who promises to work all things together for good. We have the High King who only gives good gifts. While it's true that this sovereign God does allow us to walk through difficult times and seasons, we do so with the constant assurance that He is with us and will be faithful to complete all that He has started. Immersing ourselves in the kind character of our king gives us the hope, peace, confidence, and comfort needed to live under His good rule.

> "For I am God, and there is no other; I am God, and there is none like Me, Declaring the end from the beginning,
> And from ancient times things that are not yet done,
> Saying, 'My counsel shall stand, And I will do all My pleasure'"
> Isaiah 46:9-10

Well wow, what a huge subject to tackle in just a couple of little pages. God's sovereignty has been the focused topic of endless arguments, and because of that I think we can sometimes have the tendency to shy away from talking about it. But if we look at the subject honestly, I think we'll find that we are being robbed on both ends of the radical spectrum. Those who love to make loud and adamant declarations about the sovereignty of God usually do so for the purpose of winning an argument on the point of salvation. And the ones who don't want to argue about it often miss what a beautiful attribute His sovereignty truly is. God's sovereignty is not an all-powerful control that He holds angrily above us. It's the truth of an assurance that the God who promises to work all things together for His good purpose is in absolute control. Balanced with our free will, we have the promise of His goodness in His sovereignty when we choose to serve Him, obey Him, and to live life walking along His paths. We can choose instead to spend our lives bucking up against His control, against His ways, and against His will, but like God told Saul of Tarsus, it's a hard life that is spent kicking against those goads! Does God have a will? Absolutely! He has made His sovereign declarations of what will happen to an obedient life that is spent basking in His goodness, and what will happen to a life that is spent always trying to forge its own path against His. It's our choice which side of the sovereignty of God we choose to dwell on.

I've always been taught that when I don't know something, to focus rather on what I do know. So instead of taking the time to focus here on all that we don't know about God's sovereignty towards salvation in conjunction with man's free will, let's focus on what we do know. We do know that God is King of kings and LORD of lords. We do know that He is Alpha and Omega, the Beginning and the End. We do know that He owns the earth and the fullness therein. We do know that His very Presence commands praise. We do know that He works outside of our timetables, outside of our understanding, and at times outside of our ignorant desires. We do know that our times are in His hands. We do know that His ways are high above ours. We do know that His wisdom is beyond our finding out. We do know that none can understand His plans from beginning to end. We do know that one day in heaven we will declare all of His ways to be righteous, faithful, and true. We also know that there is none other like Him. Sometimes I view the sovereignty of God as though He were an all-powerful 'me.' I tend to think that He thinks like me, makes decisions like me, acts like me, and is essentially just a mightier, unstoppable version of me. But there is *none* like Him. God doesn't act out of self-preservation, selfish tendencies, self-focus, or self-introspection like we have the propensity toward. He doesn't make decisions out of annoyance, bad moods, bad days, or dislike, as we sometimes do. He doesn't make the decisions that we would make if we had absolute control. There is none like Him!

In light of God's loving character, we have the confidence that every sovereign decision that is made is done so to be an ultimate blessing for us someday. Knowing God's character dispels all fear of the One reigning over us. We can trust and rest in His hands, knowing that every moment that touches us is filtered by His care. How have you been blessed by God's sovereignty in your life?

> "Evening and morning and at noon I will pray, and cry aloud, and He shall hear my voice."
> Psalm 55:17

Magnify!
God's Sovereignty

> "But our God is in heaven; He does whatever He pleases."
> Psalm 115:3

> "O LORD, the God of our ancestor Israel, may you be praised forever and ever! Yours, O LORD, is the greatness, the power, the glory, the victory, and the majesty. Everything in the heavens and on earth is yours, O LORD, and this is your kingdom. We adore you as the one who is over all things. Wealth and honor come from you alone, for you rule over everything. Power and might are in your hand, and at your discretion people are made great and given strength. O our God, we thank you and praise your glorious name!"
> 1 Chronicles 29:10-13 (NLT)

> "And we know that God causes everything to work together for the good of those who love God and are called according to his purpose for them."
> Romans 8:28 (NLT)

> "'For my thoughts are not your thoughts, neither are your ways my ways,' declares the LORD. 'As the heavens are higher than the earth, so are my ways higher than your ways and my thoughts than your thoughts.'"
> Isaiah 55:8-9 (ESV)

> "Who is he who speaks and it comes to pass, when the Lord has not commanded it? Is it not from the mouth of the Most High That woe and well-being proceed?"
> Lamentations 3:37-38

"Then Job answered the LORD and said: 'I know that You can do everything, And that no purpose of Yours can be withheld from You. You asked, 'Who is this who hides counsel without knowledge?' Therefore I have uttered what I did not understand, things too wonderful for me, which I did not know. Listen, please, and let me speak; You said, 'I will question you, and you shall answer Me.' I have heard of You by the hearing of the ear, but now my eye sees You. Therefore I abhor myself, and repent in dust and ashes."
Job 42:1-6

"The LORD has established His throne in the heaven, and His kingdom rules over all."
Psalm 103:19

"for it is God who works in you to will and to act in order to fulfill his good purpose."
Philippians 2:13 (NIV)

"I blessed the Most High and praised and honored Him who lives forever: For His dominion is an everlasting dominion, and His kingdom is from generation to generation. All the inhabitants of the earth are reputed as nothing; He does according to His will in the army of heaven and among the inhabitants of the earth.
No one can restrain His hand
Or say to Him, 'What have You done?'"
Daniel 4:34-35

"For I know that the LORD is great, and our Lord is above all gods. Whatever the LORD pleases He does, in heaven and in earth, In the seas and in all deep places."
Psalm 135:5-6

"He is the image of the invisible God, the firstborn over all creation. For by Him all things were created that are in heaven and that are on earth, visible and invisible, whether thrones or dominions or principalities or powers. All things were created through Him and for Him. And He is before all things, and in Him all things consist. And He is the head of the body, the church, who is the beginning, the firstborn from the dead, that in all things
He may have the preeminence."
Colossians 1:15-18

> "Enter into His gates with thanksgiving, and into His courts with praise. Be thankful to Him, and bless His name.
> For the LORD is good; His mercy is everlasting, and His truth endures to all generations."
> Psalm 100:4-5

Thank You Jesus today for…

Day 22
Magnify!
Refuge

One summer we took a vacation onboard a giant cruise ship. Everything felt plenty spacious until you had to wait in the line to get on or off the ship! Five thousand people is still five thousand people, no matter how you spread them out. During one of the beautiful island beach days, clouds began to move in, wind began to howl, and rain began to pour. As everyone was quickly trying to make their way back to the ship, the island began to flood a bit. Thunder and lightning started crashing around us, which caused people to start running toward the docks. When we finally got near the ship it was an awful sight. The line to get in must have been at least a thousand people long. We stood there lined up in the pouring rain with lightning striking around us for close to an hour before it was finally our turn to get back onboard. Humanly speaking, the crew did the best job possible of getting us all on the ship as quickly as they were able. But as I think about the word *refuge*, how much greater is it that we have a non-human, all-powerful God who is truly our refuge. There is never a line to get into His Presence. There's no waiting period to find the peace, safety, shelter, or refuge that He offers. He is our ever-present Help in time of need, and we can run to Him at any moment to find the grace and mercy that we so desperately desire.

"Be merciful to me, O God, be merciful to me!
For my soul trusts in You; And in the shadow of Your wings I will make my refuge, Until these calamities have passed by. I will cry out to God Most High, To God who performs all things for me.
He shall send from heaven and save me"
Psalm 57:1-3

Our God is a saving God. He doesn't promise a calamity free life, but He does promise to be the Refuge we can take shelter in until the calamities have passed. The rain will come, and the wind will blow, but God promises that when we cry out to Him, He will be our hiding place, refuge, high rock, and strong tower. Regardless of what is going on outwardly, inwardly we can be filled with peace by the power of His Spirit, His Word, and prayer. Our minds can be peaceful as we choose to trust in God and think upon Him. Our hearts can be steadfast as we choose to recite His word within our thoughts rather than sinking under the desperation of the wind and the waves.

Proverbs tells us that the name of God is a strong tower, and the righteous can run into it to obtain safety. There's something so sweet, soothing, comforting, and calming about just saying the name of Jesus over and over again. God's Word is filled with His different names that were given to us with the purpose of humankind finding refuge in the unique attributes of God that come along with each Name. When we fear lack, we have refuge in the assurance that God is Jehovah Jireh, our Provider. When we fear weakness, we have refuge in the assurance that God is El Roi, the Strong One who sees. When we feel the temporariness of life creeping in with fear, we have refuge in the assurance that God is El Olam, the Everlasting God. When we feel brought low and fear our own inadequacies, we have refuge in the assurance that God is El Elyon, God Most High. When we feel lost in our identity, place, and belonging we have the refuge in the assurance that God is Jehovah Nissi, the Lord My Banner, and that His banner over us is love. When we fear sickness or death, we have refuge in the assurance that God is Jehovah Rapha, God who heals. When we fear being alone we have refuge in the assurance that God is Jehovah Shammah, the God who is present. When we feel powerless and fear the limitations of our humanity, we have refuge in the assurance that God is El Shaddai and Elohim, the God Almighty of power and might. When we feel fear and anxiety deep within us, we have refuge in the assurance that God is Jehovah Shalom, the Lord our peace. When we have fear of not knowing the way to take, we have refuge in the assurance that God is Adonai, God our Master who has promised to make His way clear before our seeking sight.

What a mighty refuge we find in His name! What a mighty refuge we find in choosing to lift our thoughts into His very character and to immerse ourselves into every attribute that His character possesses. No wonder David cried out multiple times throughout Psalms, declaring the glorious refuge that our God is! Whether being chased through the wilderness, sitting atop a throne, or every tiny detail in the middle, the need we have for God to be our refuge never changes.

Is there a storm that you have been trying to weather on your own, forgetting that you have refuge, strength, and an ever-present help in time of need? Don't try to carry these burdens of life alone. Run to your Refuge and find what you're longing for today. Maybe choose one of the names of God that identifies with the place of your heart today. Write it down or carry it in your thoughts as a remembrance of the Refuge that you can run to in time of need.

*"Evening and morning and at noon I will pray, and cry aloud,
and He shall hear my voice."*
Psalm 55:17

Magnify!
Refuge

"The eternal God is your refuge, and his everlasting
arms are under you.
He drives out the enemy before you"
Deuteronomy 33:27 (NLT)

"The LORD is my rock, my fortress, and my savior; my God is
my rock, in whom I find protection. He is my shield,
the power that saves me, and my place of safety.
He is my refuge, my savior, the one who saves me from violence.
I called on the LORD, who is worthy of praise,
and he saved me from my enemies."
2 Samuel 22:2-4 (NLT)

"The LORD is a shelter for the oppressed, a refuge in times of trouble.
Those who know your name trust in you,
for you, O LORD, do not abandon those who search for you."
Psalm 9:9-10 (NLT)

"You evildoers frustrate the plans of the poor,
but the LORD is their refuge."
Psalm 14:6 (NIV)

"God also bound himself with an oath, so that those who received the
promise could be perfectly sure that he would never change his mind. So
God has given both his promise and his oath. These two things are
unchangeable because it is impossible for God to lie. Therefore, we who
have fled to him for refuge can have great confidence
as we hold to the hope that lies before us.
This hope is a strong and trustworthy anchor for our souls.
It leads us through the curtain into God's inner sanctuary."
Hebrews 6:17-19 (NLT)

"God is our refuge and strength, A very present help in trouble.
Therefore we will not fear, even though the earth be removed,
And though the mountains be carried into the midst of the sea;
Though its waters roar and be troubled,
Though the mountains shake with its swelling. Selah"
Psalm 46:1-3

"Whoever fears the LORD has a secure fortress,
and for their children it will be a refuge."
Proverbs 14:26 (NIV)

"Let all that I am wait quietly before God,
for my hope is in him. He alone is my rock and my salvation,
my fortress where I will not be shaken. My victory and honor
come from God alone. He is my refuge,
a rock where no enemy can reach me.
O my people, trust in him at all times.
Pour out your heart to him, for God is our refuge."
Psalm 62:5-8 (NLT)

"LORD, You are my strength and fortress,
my refuge in the day of trouble!"
Jeremiah 16:19 (NLT)

"But you are a tower of refuge to the poor, O LORD,
a tower of refuge to the needy in distress. You are a
refuge from the storm and a shelter from the heat.
For the oppressive acts of ruthless people are like a storm
beating against a wall, or like the relentless heat of the desert.
But you silence the roar of foreign nations. As the shade of a cloud
cools relentless heat, so the boastful songs of
ruthless people are stilled."
Isaiah 25:4-5 (NLT)

"Those who live in the shelter of the Most High will find rest
in the shadow of the Almighty. This I declare about the LORD:
he alone is my refuge, my place of safety;
he is my God, and I trust him."
Psalm 91:1-2 (NLT)

> "Enter into His gates with thanksgiving, and into His courts with praise. Be thankful to Him, and bless His name. For the LORD is good; His mercy is everlasting, and His truth endures to all generations."
> Psalm 100:4-5

Thank You Jesus today for…

_____
_____
_____
_____
_____
_____
_____
_____
_____
_____
_____
_____
_____
_____
_____
_____
_____
_____
_____
_____
_____
_____
_____
_____
_____
_____
_____
_____

Day 23
Magnify!
His Goodness

What does it mean when we say that God is good? And what do we do with the times when it doesn't feel like He is good? We know logically that He's good. But I'm sure at one time or another we would all agree that life hasn't felt good… so what do we do with that? When finances are lost, loved ones die, sickness comes upon us, and hearts are broken or crushed, how do we reconcile our feelings of God's seeming lack of goodness with the truth of His stated goodness? The book of Psalms tells us that God only does wondrous things, but what do we do when that promised truth doesn't seem to line up with the reality of our lives? I love the old phrase, "When we don't know, we fall back on what we do know," and I think that's the perfect phrase to apply to this. We don't know why God chooses to do what He does, or how He can deem something "good" that seems as polar opposite from goodness as you can get. But there are things about God's goodness that we *do* know, and that's what I would love for us to magnify today.

"And the Holy Spirit helps us in our weakness. For example, we don't know what God wants us to pray for. But the Holy Spirit prays for us with groanings that cannot be expressed in words. And the Father who knows all hearts knows what the Spirit is saying, for the Spirit pleads for us believers in harmony with God's own will. And we know that God causes everything to work together for the good of those who love God and are called according to his purpose for them."
Romans 8:26-28 (NLT)

What if I asked you if you wanted a big spoonful of sodium potassium? Would you take it? Or would you want a bowl full of lithium? I would assume the answer to both of those offers is going to be a resounding, "No!" Yet, I'm sure you know that if you take both of those components, neither of which are good in and of themselves, and you mix them with chlorine, you get one of the most glorious table elements out there. Salt! I'm a salt lover, and I can say that though I would never choose to eat sodium potassium or lithium alone, together I can't live without them. So often I hear the question when bad things happen, "How could God call this good?" While my heart breaks with people in their tragedy, the truth is that God doesn't say everything that happens *is* good. He says that He will *work* it together for good. In the same way that the table salt elements are not good in and of themselves, with some working together they *become* good. Tragic happenings and hard times are not good in and of themselves, but combined with God's grace, goodness, faithfulness, and steadfastness love, they are worked together for the ultimate good of His plan for us.

I really can't stand exercising, and yet I know how good it is for me. In reality, it sure doesn't feel good in the moment, does it? Some of you crazy ones might say, "YES! It feels great!" But I think the majority of us would say, "NO! It feels awful in the moment!" But the phrase, "in the moment," is such an important one. Exercise seems like an un-good thing that leaves us feeling weak, shaky, and sweaty. When I exercise my legs feel like rubber, my heart feels like it's about to burst out of my chest, and I'm so tired that I can hardly see straight. (And that's why I rarely ever exercise! Ha!) But you 'fit' people would argue that if I just kept at it I would feel stronger and healthier! Now before you close this book, confused on whether this is a devotional or an exercise manual, I want to say the word, "SAME!" Trials have the same concept and produce the same result as exercise. Though trials feel AWFUL in the moment, and leave us feeling weak like rubber, sweaty with panic, and so tired we can hardly think straight, they will eventually leave us feeling stronger, healthier, and more alive. If I ever met with a physical trainer, (and I'm fairly sure that will *never* happen) I would be tempted to feel like the pain was a personal attack. Hopefully, I would instead have the understanding that every painful exercise I was instructed to partake in was for the ultimate goal of the desired healthy body. God is working within us a far greater weight of glory than we could ever imagine or understand. As our Heavenly Personal Trainer, He is working the trials for good within us. Spiritual muscles never feel good while they're forming, but we can trust that it's not a wasted effort, and that it's not intended to harm us. Strength will come through what seems to be weakening us, and the hard times will all be worked for good within our lives.

All in all, we just simply can't understand God. He actually declares that His ways are higher than ours and that we won't be able to figure Him out. I would love for it to be a trite answer of why God doesn't always seem good, or a quick-fix plan to see the good in everything. I would love for life to be easy, for there to be no bad days, and for everything to always seem good. But maybe the point of difficult times and trials is to loosen the roots of our lives that would otherwise tend to go deep and lock in firm. We're not citizens of this world. This place is not our home. This life won't last forever. And maybe every painful thing in this life is just a reminder and an encouragement to press on toward our heavenly home, where every tear is wiped away forever by the good hand of God. And I think we would all agree that life in heaven will be a GOOD thing.

"Evening and morning and at noon I will pray, and cry aloud, and He shall hear my voice."
Psalm 55:17

Magnify!
His Goodness

"Taste and see that the LORD is good.
Oh, the joys of those who take refuge in him!"
Psalm 34:8 (NLT)

"But you, Lord, are a compassionate and gracious God,
slow to anger, abounding in love and faithfulness."
Psalm 86:15 (NIV)

"Whatever is good and perfect is a gift coming down to us from God
our Father, who created all the lights in the heavens.
He never changes or
casts a shifting shadow."
James 1:17 (NLT)

"Surely goodness and mercy shall follow me All the days of my life;
And I will dwell in the house of the LORD Forever."
Psalm 23:6

"The LORD replied to Moses, "I will indeed do what you have asked, for I look favorably on you, and I know you by name." Moses responded, "Then show me your glorious presence." The LORD replied, "I will make all my goodness pass before you, and I will call out my name, Yahweh, before you. For I will show mercy to anyone I choose, and I will show compassion to anyone I choose."
Exodus 33:17-19 (NLT)

"The LORD is good to everyone.
He showers compassion on all his creation."
Psalm 145:9 (NLT)

"You are good, and what you do is good; teach me your decrees."
Psalm 119:68 (NIV)

"No one is good except God alone."
Mark 10:18

"I would have lost heart, unless I had believed That I would see the goodness of the LORD In the land of the living."
Psalm 27:13

"Give thanks to the LORD, for he is good;
his love endures forever."
1 Chronicles 16:34 (NIV)

"The LORD is good, a strong refuge when trouble comes.
He is close to those who trust in him."
Nahum 1:7 (NLT)

"Like newborn babies, crave pure spiritual milk, so that by it you may grow up in your salvation, now that you have tasted
that the Lord is good."
1 Peter 2:2-3 (NIV)

"Oh give thanks to the LORD, for he is good,
for his steadfast love endures forever!"
Psalm 107:1 (ESV)

"For I know the plans I have for you," says the LORD. "They are plans for good and not for disaster, to give you a future and a hope."
Jeremiah 29:11 (NLT)

"How great is the goodness you have stored up for those who fear you. You lavish it on those who come to you for protection,
blessing them before the watching world."
Psalm 31:19 (NLT)

"For the LORD God is our sun and our shield. He gives us grace and glory. The LORD will withhold no good thing
from those who do what is right."
Psalm 84:11 (NLT)

"With praise and thanksgiving they sang to the LORD: "He is good; his love toward Israel endures forever." And all the people gave a great shout of praise to the LORD, because the
foundation of the house of the LORD was laid."
Ezra 3:11 (NIV)

"Enter into His gates with thanksgiving, and into His courts with praise. Be thankful to Him, and bless His name. For the LORD is good; His mercy is everlasting, and His truth endures to all generations."
Psalm 100:4-5

Thank You Jesus today for…

Day 24
Magnify!
His Miracles

I've been in the Galilee area for the last few days as I write this, and I just can't stop thinking about how many miracles Jesus performed in this small area of Israel. From morning till night, normal days to Sabbath days, whether He was weary, tired or hungry, His eyes were constantly looking out for those who needed His touch. He was always drawn to the one with the greatest need. Regardless of His own condition He was moved with the compassion of the Father to the sheep who were in desperate need of the Good Shepherd. I can't wrap my mind around all the lives that were drastically changed in this very place.

> "And Jesus did many other signs in the presence of His disciples, which are not written in this book; but these are written that you may believe that Jesus is the Christ, the Son of God, and that believing you may have life in His name."
> John 20:30-31 (ESV)

> "And there are also many other things that Jesus did, which if they were written one by one, I suppose that even the world itself could not contain the books that would be written. Amen."
> John 21:25

Sitting here, overlooking the water and thinking about the countless storms that were calmed and the countless precious ones who found the touch of Jesus in their time of need is overwhelming to me. Just think about the ones who were plunged into need because of their own sin. The paralytic was lowered down from a roof not far from here. His friends had brought him so that he could walk again, and yet Jesus knew that the greatest need of his heart was to be cleansed from the haunting past of his sin. His newfound purity came with renewed legs that showed the world that the Son of Man had the power to forgive sin. Maybe you or someone you know has a story of sin having a grip that could only be loosed by the freeing words of Jesus, who has the power to forgive, cleanse, pardon, and raise up.

I'm thinking of the blind who had greater eyesight than some of those who could see; the ones who knew that if they could just reach out to Jesus then their begging days would be over, and their eyesight would be renewed. Could you imagine what it must have been like to walk in the dark for years upon years and then at the touch of Jesus, the spit of Jesus, the mud of Jesus, or just at the very word of Jesus, suddenly you could see what you could never see before? Their lives would be changed forever! They could see the faces of loved ones, foods they had only smelled, colors they could never have imagined, and every object that belonged to every noise they had ever heard. Maybe there's a blindness that needs to be lifted up in prayer today. The touch of Jesus can give sight to the blind, sight to the heart, and sight where there has been only darkness.

My heart is dwelling with every broken parent who was made whole in this place, from the father of the demon possessed son to the father of the sick little girl. I'm living out the emotions of the mom of the demon possessed daughter that Jesus healed, and the widowed mom with the dead son Jesus raised to life. Could you imagine the pain and the suffering they had gone through, and the desperation that they must have run to Jesus with? Was it their last effort? Was it their final glimmer of hope? The precious widow with the dead son didn't even reach out to Jesus- He noticed her! He reached out to her! He raised her son from the dead without her even asking Him to! Is there a child, a person, a loved one, or a friend that you need to reach out to Jesus on behalf of today? He longs to bring healing.

I'm wondering how every leper felt. They had such difficult lives. The moment a priest pronounced them unclean every aspect of the life they had known would be changed for the worse. They would no longer be allowed to live near their family. They would never feel the touch of another human without causing them to become unclean. They would begin to waste away until finally rotting to death. And yet, this beautiful, brave Jesus reached out to touch the skin that had been pronounced untouchable. Jesus healed what could never have been healed by another. He restored not only their bodies but made their lives new as well. Is there a sin that you have watched eat a life away? Jesus longs to touch what none other has been able to touch with His healing hands.

My eyes are longing to see the scene where the woman unclean with her issue of blood crawled on the ground, desperate to stay out of sight to the crowd, but even more desperate to touch the hem of His garment and be made well. Exposed by Jesus so that He could declare her clean, she was never the same again. Is there a desperate situation that needs His touch and His healing today?

Our God is a living and powerful God who is awake with passion toward us and desperate to heal, touch, restore, and raise to life more areas of our lives than we would ever have time to list. Would we be those who spread our stories that are filled with the wonder working power of our mighty Savior!

"Evening and morning and at noon I will pray, and cry aloud, and He shall hear my voice."
Psalm 55:17

Magnify!
His Miracles

"Now there were set there six waterpots of stone, according to the manner of purification of the Jews, containing twenty or thirty gallons apiece. Jesus said to them, 'Fill the waterpots with water.' And they filled them up to the brim. And He said to them, 'Draw some out now, and take it to the master of the feast.' And they took it. When the master of the feast had tasted the water that was made wine, and did not know where it came from but the servants who had drawn the water knew"
John 2:6-10

"So Jesus came again to Cana of Galilee where He had made the water wine. And there was a certain nobleman whose son was sick at Capernaum. When he heard that Jesus had come out of Judea into Galilee, he went to Him and implored Him to come down and heal his son, for he was at the point of death. Then Jesus said to him, 'Unless you people see signs and wonders, you will by no means believe.' The nobleman said to Him, 'Sir, come down before my child dies!' Jesus said to him, 'Go your way; your son lives.' So the man believed the word that Jesus spoke to him, and he went his way. And as he was now going down, his servants met him and told him, saying, 'Your son lives!' Then he inquired of them the hour when he got better. And they said to him, 'Yesterday at the seventh hour the fever left him.' So the father knew that it was at the same hour in which Jesus said to him, 'Your son lives.' And he himself believed, and his whole household."
John 4:46-54

"When He had stopped speaking, He said to Simon, 'Launch out into the deep and let down your nets for a catch.' But Simon answered and said to Him, 'Master we have toiled all night and caught nothing; nevertheless at Your word I will let down the net.' And when they had done this, they caught a great number of fish, and their net was breaking. So they signaled to their partners in the other boat to come and help them. And they came and filled both the boats, so that they began to sink. When Simon Peter saw it, he fell down at Jesus' knees, saying, 'Depart from me, for I am a sinful man, O Lord!'"
Luke 5:4-8

"Now as soon as they had come out of the synagogue, they entered
the house of Simon and Andrew, with James and John.
But Simon's wife's mother lay sick with a fever,
and they told Him about her at once.
So He came and took her by the hand and lifted her up,
and immediately the fever left her. And she served them.
At evening, when the sun had set, they brought to Him
all who were sick and those who were demon-possessed.
And the whole city was gathered together at the door.
Then He healed many who were sick with various diseases,
and cast out many demons; He did not allow the demons to speak,
because they knew Him."
Mark 1:29-34

"And when He was already not far from the house,
the centurion sent friends to Him, saying to Him,
'Lord, do not trouble Yourself, for I am not worthy that
You should enter under my roof. Therefore I did not even think
myself worthy to come to You. But say the word,
and my servant will be healed… When Jesus heard these things,
He marveled at him… And those who were sent, returning to the
house, found the servant well who had been sick."
Luke 7:6-8, 9, 10

"When the Lord saw her, He had compassion on her and said to her,
'Do not weep.' Then He came and touched the open coffin,
and those who carried him stood still. And He said,
'Young man, I say to you, arise.' So he who was dead
sat up and began to speak.
And He presented him to his mother."
Luke 7:13-15

"And when He had come into the house, the blind men came to Him.
And Jesus said to them, 'Do you believe that I am able to do this?'
They said to Him, 'Yes, Lord.' Then He touched their eyes,
saying, 'According to your faith let it be to you.'
And their eyes were opened."
Matthew 9:28-30

> "Enter into His gates with thanksgiving, and into His courts with praise. Be thankful to Him, and bless His name. For the LORD is good; His mercy is everlasting, and His truth endures to all generations."
>
> Psalm 100:4-5

Thank You Jesus today for…

Day 25
Magnify!
The Priest

From the beginning, God wanted nothing to come between Him and His people. People were created naked, open, and vulnerable before the Living God. It wasn't until sin entered the world that the first covering was put into place, the first hiding was done, and the first human-to-God separation existed. God created His people to walk with Him in humble, open obedience and surrender. When sin entered the picture, the damage was done. There was no turning around. There was no going back. There was no undoing what was done. Sin and consequences had taken root. But Jesus is the Lamb slain before the foundation of the world. Before the first bite was taken, before the first step was taken toward a hiding place, before the first fig leaf was taken and sewn, Jesus was on His way to the cross so that all communion could be eternally restored, all sin could be wiped away, all death and destruction could be done away with, and our souls could live in full surrender and harmony once again within the shadow of the Presence of God.

"Therefore, since we have a great High Priest who has ascended into heaven, Jesus the Son of God, let us hold firmly to the faith we profess. For we do not have a high priest who is unable to empathize with our weaknesses, but we have one who has been tempted in every way, just as we are- yet he did not sin. Let us then approach God's throne of grace with confidence, so that we may receive mercy and find grace to help us in our time of need."
Hebrews 4:14-16 (NIV)

When God formed His nation upon bringing them out of Israel, He set priestly practices into motion. The office of priest was given by God because He wanted those who would stand in the gap between His holiness and the sinfulness of man. Unable to stop sinning on our own, we were hopelessly lost and desperately destitute with no way of cleaning ourselves up, changing our habits, or cleansing our sin-stained minds. Guilt separates. If it isn't our own guilty conscience that calls us to distance ourselves from God, then the whispers of the enemy sure do the trick. From the beginning of the priesthood, God was designing His people to run *into* His Presence anytime sin took hold of their lives. Our knee-jerk reaction is to run *from* the Presence of God. It's what Adam and Eve did, and it's what we feel the propensity toward as well. We feel the guilt and shame. We feel the embarrassment of the wanting to be better, yet we have no idea how to attain to that place of "better." We feel the regret of falling once again into the sin, patterns, and habits that we were just sure we were strong enough to stay out of this time. And so, the sacrifices were instituted. The office of priest was formed. The guilt offerings were followed, and the burnt offerings were initiated. Why? Why the sacrifices? Why the offerings? Why the rituals in the temple? Surely watching the life drain out of an animal didn't ease a guilty conscience. We're told in the book of Hebrews that the blood of bulls and goats could never take away our sin. So why the sacrifices? Maybe because our gracious God knew our tendency to stay in the shadows of our committed sin, too embarrassed and ashamed to come into His Presence with the words, "Hey God, it's me, and I did it again." God instead instituted within His people a habit to resist hiding and to instead run into His Presence for cleansing. The priest was to be the go-between, the mediator, the one who set in place new beginnings. The priest was to be the one with the messages of grace, forgiveness, newness, redemption, rightness, renewal, and revival.

Jesus entered earth as the gracious God who laid aside His deity to pick up our humanity, so that He could be our sympathetic High Priest. He understands our weakness, our frailty, our temptations, our failings, our floundering's, and our struggles. He lived out this life of humanity to the highest degree of spotless perfection. Jesus stands now as our Mediator. We are seen as spotless, sinless, forgiven, washed clean, redeemed, and made new! He stands as a Representative of the life that we could never live. He stands as our entrance into heaven, our door into salvation, our Redeemer, our Resurrection, and our Life. He stands as the only One whose blood could make us truly clean, the only One who could set us truly free, and the only One who could truly satisfy the righteous standard of perfection. True to the calling of a priest, He stands before us on God's behalf. He stands before us to declare the messages of God's never-changing, never-ending, higher-than-the-sky love. He stands before us to declare that the redemption plan was formed before the foundation of the world because this all-loving God desired that we wouldn't spend one moment outside of His Presence. This Father chose a moment of separation from His Son so that you and I would never need to feel a moment of separation from Him.

Jesus is our great High Priest who came to burst open the Holy of Holies so that we could run unobstructed and obtain that mercy we so desperately needed. He came to be the Mediator; our go-between. But even greater than the human priests who could smooth out our sins out for a time, Jesus came as the Spotless Lamb and Great High Priest who could remove our sins for all of eternity! Hallelujah to the High Priest who could take away our sin and shame!

"Evening and morning and at noon I will pray, and cry aloud, and He shall hear my voice."
Psalm 55:17

Magnify!
The Priest

"Coming to Him as to a living stone, rejected indeed by men, but chosen by God and precious, you also, as living stones, are being built up a spiritual house, a holy priesthood, to offer up spiritual sacrifices acceptable to God through Jesus Christ....But you are a chosen generation, a royal priesthood, a holy nation, His own special people, that you may proclaim the praises of Him who called you out of darkness into His marvelous light"
1 Peter 2:4-5, 9

"And they sang a new song, saying: "You are worthy to take the scroll and to open its seals, because you were slain, and with your blood you purchased for God persons from every tribe and language and people and nation. You have made them to be a kingdom and priests to serve our God, and they will reign on the earth.""
Revelation 5:9-10 (NIV)

"So guard yourselves and God's people. Feed and shepherd God's flock—his church, purchased with his own blood— over which the Holy Spirit has appointed you as leaders."
Acts 20:28 (NLT)

"True instruction was in his mouth and nothing false was found on his lips. He walked with me in peace and uprightness, and turned many from sin. For the lips of a priest ought to preserve knowledge, because he is the messenger of the LORD Almighty and people seek instruction from his mouth. But you have turned from the way and by your teaching have caused many to stumble; you have violated the covenant with Levi," says the LORD Almighty. "So I have caused you to be despised and humiliated before all the people, because you have not followed my ways but have shown partiality in matters of the law."
Malachi 2:6-9 (NIV)

"To Him who loved us and washed us from our sins in His own blood, and has made us kings and priests to His God and Father, to Him be glory and dominion forever and ever. Amen."
Revelation 1:5-6

"Blessed and holy are those who share in the first resurrection. For them the second death holds no power, but they will be priests of God and of Christ and will reign with him a thousand years."
Revelation 20:6 (NLT)

"We have this hope as an anchor for the soul, firm and secure. It enters the inner sanctuary behind the curtain, where our forerunner, Jesus, has entered on our behalf. He has become a high priest forever, in the order of Melchizedek."
Hebrews 6:19-20 (NIV)

"Every high priest is selected from among the people and is appointed to represent the people in matters related to God, to offer gifts and sacrifices for sins. He is able to deal gently with those who are ignorant and are going astray, since he himself is subject to weakness. This is why he has to offer sacrifices for his own sins, as well as for the sins of the people. And no one takes this honor on himself, but he receives it when called by God, just as Aaron was. In the same way, Christ did not take on himself the glory of becoming a high priest. But God said to him, "You are my Son; today I have become Your Father." And he says in another place, "You are a priest forever, in the order of Melchizedek."
During the days of Jesus' life on earth, he offered up prayers and petitions with fervent cries and tears to the one who could save him from death, and he was heard because of his reverent submission. Son though he was, he learned obedience from what he suffered and, once made perfect, he became the source of eternal salvation for all who obey him and was designated by God to be high priest
in the order of Melchizedek."
Hebrews 5:1-10 (NIV)

"For this reason he had to be made like them, fully human in every way, in order that he might become a merciful and faithful high priest in service to God, and that he might make atonement for the sins of the people. Because he himself suffered when he was tempted, he is able to help those who are being tempted."
Hebrews 2:17 (NIV)

"Enter into His gates with thanksgiving, and into His courts with praise. Be thankful to Him, and bless His name. For the LORD is good; His mercy is everlasting, and His truth endures to all generations."
Psalm 100:4-5

Thank You Jesus today for…

Day 26
Magnify!
His Holiness

Have you ever had someone rebuke you for a failure or a shortcoming? I remember one day being confronted by someone about how I hadn't measured up to who she expected me to be. She told me all the ways I was failing people and falling short. I was devastated. On one hand I felt like the accusations were unjustified, but on the other hand, it took days to shake the overwhelming feeling of not being enough in someone's eyes. In those days the tender words of Jesus came to my heart to remind me that my feelings were true. I was not enough and could never be enough, and that's why I needed Him! Even more beautiful and reassuring was His reminder that He never expected me to be enough. What is it about us that knows we could never earn salvation on our own, but then expects ourselves and those around us to walk the line of sanctification perfectly? God expects one thing out of us. He expects us to never measure up. That's why He came Himself! He's the only One good enough, righteous enough, and holy enough to ever measure up to His perfect standards that we frequently put on ourselves and others.

"The LORD said to Moses, 'You shall also make a basin of bronze, with its stand of bronze, for washing. You shall put it between the tent of meeting and the altar, and you shall put water in it, with which Aaron and his sons shall wash their hands and their feet. When they go into the tent of meeting, or when they come near the altar to minister, to burn a food offering to the LORD, they shall wash with water, so they may not die. They shall wash their hands and their feet, so that they may not die. It shall be a statue forever to them"
Exodus 30:17-21 (ESV)

When my children were little we had a lightly colored carpet that just seemed to attract a new stain with each new day. Sometimes our lives can feel a bit like that old worn out carpet. We want to be good. We want to help people. We want to live righteously, but it just feels like our lives are only magnifying our own failures, stains, and shortcomings. God called His priests to have a basin to wash themselves in, right in between the place of God's Presence and the place where they ministered on behalf of man. In order for there to be a human place of ministry, there had to be a place of holy cleansing and washing.

God's standard of holiness is one that we could never measure up to on our own. We could never attain to His perfection, yet He still desires to use imperfect us! Knowing that His priests could never come before His Presence without the shadow of imperfection upon them, God set up a way for them to symbolically wash themselves clean in His sight in order for them to be useful to His people. In the same way, we'll always be imperfect in ministry and life. And yet God, in His gracious holiness, has also provided a way to wash us clean from the stains we incur day to day. How wonderful it is to have our minds, hearts, and memories washed clean by the water of God's Word and through the power of the Holy Spirit. We could never wash ourselves clean enough for salvation, but salvation wasn't the purpose of the priest's washing basin in Exodus. They were to wash for service, for usefulness, for cleanliness, for obedience, and for holiness. We need to be washed by the water of God's Word and Spirit so that we can be rid of our day-to-day filth and be used by God to reflect His glory and beauty to others.

Without God we have no way to wash our souls. Without His cleansing we have no way to live for Him in an effective and useful way. There is none good but Him. He is the Everlasting Holy God, not us! God is the only One who is surrounded by heavenly creatures singing His praise and constantly declaring His holiness. God is the only One who is worthy of the worship of others. There is nothing that you or I could ever do on our own to ever measure up to His righteous standard or His holy ways. Without our feet and our hands washed by His holy grace there is not one useful thing that we could ever do in this life. Our own righteousness is like filthy rags, and what a glorious sigh of relief that should bring to us. His throne is the one we worship at, not our own. His name is the one we exalt, not our own. It's all His water, His basin, and His glorious Presence that can wash us with any kind of holiness. It should amaze us that He enables us to do anything right at all!

More than likely, we won't ever get to the place where we stop letting people down. We won't ever be able to live perfectly, perfectly meet their expectations, or do ministry according to the standards of their opinions. But praise God we weren't designed to live a life that pleases people. How funny it is that sinful humanity is more difficult to please than the Holy God! Praise be to God for washing us clean with salvation and washing our stained moments each day through His Word and the power of the Holy Spirit. Regardless of the standards of man, His is one of perfection, and He alone has made a way for us to stand before His throne in blamelessness. God alone is worthy of worship. So next time someone lets you know that you are less than enough, let them know they're right, shake it off in prayer, and point their eyes to God, who alone is Holy!

"Evening and morning and at noon I will pray, and cry aloud, and He shall hear my voice."
Psalm 55:17

Magnify!
His Holiness

"Yet you are holy, O you who are enthroned upon the praises of Israel."
Psalm 22:3 (ESV)

"For thus says the high and exalted one who lives forever, whose name is Holy, 'I dwell on a high and holy place, And also with the contrite and lowly of spirit In order to revive the spirit of the lowly And to revive the heart of the contrite.'"
Isaiah 57:15 (NASB)

"The four living creatures, each having six wings, were full of eyes around and within. And they do not rest day or night, saying: 'Holy, holy, holy, Lord God Almighty, Who was and is and is to come!'"
Revelation 4:8

"Then I will praise you with music on the harp, because you are faithful to your promises, O my God. I will sing praises to you with a lyre, O Holy One of Israel."
Psalm 71:22 (NLT)

"I am the LORD, your Holy One, the Creator of Israel, your King. Thus says the LORD, who makes a way in the sea And a path through the mighty waters"
Isaiah 43:15-16

"No one is holy like the LORD, for there is none besides You, Nor is there any rock like our God."
1 Samuel 2:2

"O God, your ways are holy. Is there any god as mighty as you?"
Psalm 77:13 (NLT)

"'To whom will you compare me? Who is my equal?'
asks the Holy One."
Isaiah 40:25 (NLT)

"Who is like you among the gods, O LORD— glorious in holiness,
awesome in splendor, performing great wonders?"
Exodus 15:11 (NLT)

"Who shall not fear You, O Lord, and glorify Your name?
For You alone are holy. For all nations shall
come and worship before You"
Revelation 15:4

"Save us, O God of our salvation; Gather us together, and deliver us
from the Gentiles, To give thanks to Your holy name,
To triumph in Your praise."
1 Chronicles 16:35

"In him our hearts rejoice, for we trust in his holy name."
Psalm 33:21 (NLT)

"For He who is mighty has done great things for me,
and holy is His name."
Luke 1:49

"But the LORD is in his holy Temple.
Let all the earth be silent before him."
Habakkuk 2:20 (NLT)

"But the LORD of Heaven's Armies will be exalted by his justice.
The holiness of God will be displayed by his righteousness."
Isaiah 5:16 (NLT)

"He is the kind of high priest we need because he is holy and
blameless, unstained by sin. He has been set apart from sinners and has
been given the highest place of honor in heaven."
Hebrews 7:26 (NLT)

"but as He who called you is holy, you also be holy in
all your conduct, because it is written, 'Be holy, for I am holy.'"
1 Peter 1:15-16

> "Enter into His gates with thanksgiving, and into His courts with praise. Be thankful to Him, and bless His name. For the LORD is good; His mercy is everlasting, and His truth endures to all generations."
> Psalm 100:4-5

Thank You Jesus today for…

Day 27
Magnify!
God's Light

Do you remember the story of the ten virgins found in Matthew 25? You can read the details later if you're not sure of them, but to sum the story up: five were ready with enough oil to follow the bridegroom to the wedding feast, and five were not. The five who weren't ready were left behind as the bridegroom and those who were ready to follow him made their way to the celebration. This story breaks my heart because, at one point, these five unready girls wanted to be ready for the call to the feast! They had bought lamps and stationed themselves with the other girls who were on the invite list, so what happened? Had they forgotten what they were waiting for? Did they think they had plenty of time ahead of them to buy oil later? Did they get distracted by the busyness of the world? Did they forget that they were separated for a purpose and were meant to live ready for the call to the feast?

> "In the beginning, God created the heavens and the earth. The earth was without form and void, and darkness was over the face of the deep. And the Spirit of God was hovering over the face of the waters. And God said, 'Let there be light,' and there was light. And God saw that the light was good. And God separated the light from the darkness. God called the light Day, and the darkness he called Night."
> Genesis 1:1-5

The light of God began with separation. It began with a clear distinction from the dark. There wasn't "lightish" or "mostly not dark." Light didn't mesh with the dark and the lines weren't blurry. There was dark and there was light. God desires to take frequent evaluations of any darkness in our lives that could be drowning out His light. He wants us to be open and exposed to the floodlight of His glory; not for shame or embarrassment, but for purity and readiness. He desires to burn out of our lives those dark spots that would lead us to nothingness and hinder us from walking in the light as He is in the light. God is the Separator of light and darkness. It's His voice that calls light into being where only darkness and void has been. He is the One who floods us with His light that immediately dispels all darkness within us. As long as people of God forget that they are to live *in* the light, *for* the light, and *by* the light, there will always be those who don't have enough light to last for the journey. We are a people who are called to be flooded daily with the fire from the Holy Spirit in order have the light that is needed to follow after Him. We don't have flames of our own, oil of our own, or light in and of ourselves.

It is by His light that we see life. Our passion alone is not enough to keep our lamps lit. We need a daily filling, a daily closeness, and a daily fire that stems from intimacy with our Savior.

Have you ever been walking somewhere in the dark only to have the lights suddenly turn on? It's amazing how shadows instantly become normal objects rather than looming wonders. Maybe we fear the darkness because we don't understand His light of life within us. You don't need a lamp until it's dark. You don't need a flashlight until there is no light on the path. And maybe we wouldn't realize our great need for Jesus until the lights of circumstantial happiness dim a little. Without the darkness, maybe we wouldn't press into the light in such a passionate way. Just like on a chilly day when we press into the sunlight, maybe in the darkness of life we press into His light a little more than usual. Even as a floodlight as opposed to a keychain flashlight, we will find the Light of the World to be more than adequate for our need of light. Jesus is our Bright and morning star!

Revelation tells us that we will have no need of sun in the new Kingdom because God's glory will be the light. Can you imagine that? I wonder if we'll get a glory-tan the way we get a sun-tan here on earth! Frequent moments spent basking in earthly sunlight fills us up with all the vitamin D needed for health and vitality. In the same way, frequent moments of basking in God's light through prayer and time in His Word floods our faces with His glory as He shines forth His glory upon us. We too, like Moses, can have faces that shine from His Presence. We too, like Moses, can have the light of the Pillar of fire that leads our way through this sometimes-dark life. We too, like the men on the road to Emmaus, can have our hearts burn within us as He speaks His Words to us. Jesus is the Light of the world!

Have you ever played a game of Hide and Seek in the dark? Without God as the light of our vision, we stumble around like the blind leading the blind. It is God who gives us light for our vision. Psalm 82 reminds us that the people in this world walk about in darkness with neither knowledge nor understanding. We have the light that they desperately long for. Even if they react in animosity toward the Light that we share with them, it's still what they long for. They are desperately alone in the darkness, looking for a way out. They want to be "found." They want to come out of hiding. They want to know a better way, and they want the safety of a light. We have the light that they long for. Take a few minutes right now to pray and ask God if there's someone that He wants you to share His light of life with today!

"Evening and morning and at noon I will pray, and cry aloud, and He shall hear my voice."
Psalm 55:17

Magnify!
God's Light

"Your word is a lamp to guide my feet and
a light for my path."
Psalm 119:105 (NLT)

"Arise, shine; For your light has come!
And the glory of the LORD is risen upon you.
For behold, the darkness shall cover the earth,
And deep darkness the people; But the LORD will arise over you,
And His glory will be seen upon you.
The Gentiles shall come to your light,
And kings to the brightness of your rising."
Isaiah 60:1-3

"For you were once darkness, but now you are light in the Lord. Walk as children of light (for the fruit of the Spirit is in all goodness, righteousness, and truth), finding out what is acceptable to the Lord. And have no fellowship with the unfruitful works of darkness, but rather expose them. For it is shameful even to speak of those things which are done by them in secret. But all things that are exposed are made manifest by the light, for whatever makes manifest is light.
Therefore He says: 'Awake, you who sleep,
Arise from the dead, And Christ will give you light.'"
Ephesians 5:8-14

"No one, when he has lit a lamp, puts it in a secret place or under a basket, but on a lampstand, that those who come in may see the light. The lamp of the body is the eye. Therefore, when your eye is good, your whole body also is full of light. But when your eye is bad, your body also is full of darkness. Therefore take heed that the light which is in you is not darkness. If then your whole body is full of light, having no part dark, the whole body will be full of light,
as when the bright shining of a lamp gives you light."
Luke 11:33-36

"In the beginning was the Word, and the Word was with God, and the Word was God. He was in the beginning with God. All things were made through Him, and without Him nothing was made that was made. In Him was life, and the life was the light of men. And the light shines in the darkness, and the darkness did not comprehend it."
John 1:1-5

"The LORD is my light and my salvation;
Whom shall I fear?"
Psalm 27:1 (NIV)

"Then Jesus spoke to them again, saying, 'I am the light of the world. He who follows Me shall not walk in darkness, but have the light of life.'"
John 8:12

"The people who walked in darkness
Have seen a great light; Those who dwelt in the land of
the shadow of death,
Upon them a light has shined."
Isaiah 9:2

"This is the message which we have heard from Him and declare to you, that God is light and in Him is no darkness at all. If we say that we have fellowship with Him, and walk in darkness, we lie and do not practice the truth. But if we walk in the light as He is in the light, we have fellowship with one another, and the blood of Jesus Christ His Son cleanses us from all sin."
1 John 1:5-7

"The unfolding of your words gives light;
it gives understanding to the simple."
Psalm 119:130 (NIV)

"Then Jesus said to them, 'A little while longer the light is with you. Walk while you have the light, lest darkness overtake you; he who walks in darkness does not know where he is going. While you have the light, believe in the light, that you may become sons of light.'"
John 12:35-36

"Let your light so shine before men, that they may see your good works and glorify your Father in heaven."
Matthew 5:16

> "Enter into His gates with thanksgiving, and into His courts with praise. Be thankful to Him, and bless His name. For the LORD is good; His mercy is everlasting, and His truth endures to all generations."
> Psalm 100:4-5

Thank You Jesus today for…

_____
_____
_____
_____
_____
_____
_____
_____
_____
_____
_____
_____
_____
_____
_____
_____
_____
_____
_____
_____
_____
_____
_____
_____
_____
_____
_____

Day 28
Magnify!
The Servant

Have you ever met someone who seemed as though they thought they lived above everyone? I remember feeling such anger and astonishment while having dinner at a nice restaurant one night with a couple of friends. I couldn't believe the way one of the girls in our group was treating the server. There was no eye contact or smiling; no please or thank you. There were only the exchanges of a haughty queen toward her lowly servant. What made this moment so much worse was that we had been telling this precious server all about Jesus. It broke my heart to now watch her being treated in a way that was miles apart from the example of who Jesus truly was. Jesus the King, the Mighty One, the One who left His heavenly throne to take on the flesh of man- He was the only One ever to walk this earth who was deserving of the praise and worship of all. Yet in all of His hidden royalty, He never demanded worship. He never demanded to be treated as the high King that He was. He came to this earth and took on the form of a servant. He chose to be despised rather than worshiped, so that you and I one day could worship around His throne with multitudes of heavenly beings.

> "In your relationships with one another, have the same mindset as Christ Jesus: Who, being in very nature God, did not consider equality with God something to be used to his own advantage; rather, he made himself nothing by taking the very nature of a servant, being made in human likeness.
> And being found in appearance as a man, he humbled himself by becoming obedient to death— even death on a cross!"
> Philippians 2:5-8 (NIV)

One night while reading Luke, I noticed that there will be a point in our future where Jesus will sit us down and serve us. That concept immediately dropped me to my knees in awe. It wasn't just that Jesus took on the form of a servant here on earth, but as High King He will serve us again? That's just too much for my finite mind to take in. What if you and I had the exciting privilege of jumping on a plane headed for England to go visit the Queen? Could you imagine if we walked into Buckingham Palace and she took off her crown, put on an apron, seated us, and began to serve us dinner? We would be astonished! Sweet friend, how much more astonishing should it be to us that the King of kings and Lord of lords will don an apron and serve us in heaven! If Jesus doesn't hang onto the privilege of being served, who do we think we are to take that privilege up?

One day I was helping out at the school my kids were attending. As I watched the playground I noticed that everyone in the tetherball line kept letting my first-grade son go ahead of them. It seemed strange to me, so when we got home later that day I asked him about it, and here's how the conversation went:

Me- "Why was everyone letting you go ahead of them in the tether ball line today?"
Jonathan- "Well I just kept telling them that if they would choose to be last here on earth, then God would let them be first in heaven."
Me (shocked out of my mind) - "Won't you be sad when you get to heaven and you're last in everything?"
Jonathan- "Mom, God doesn't really care about silly little things like tetherball lines!"

Pastor's kids... Believe me when I tell you that this was a mindset that we put much effort into correcting! But honestly, I think it's a mindset that needs to be frequently corrected in us as well! We sometimes forget that we're here to live a cross-carrying life. We sometimes forget that Jesus was despised and rejected by man and warned us that as we follow Him, we would become the same. We sometimes forget that as He took off His non-kingly garment and washed the disciples' feet, He called us to do the same. I think our lives beg the frequent question, are we living to be served or to serve, because there's only one of those options that follow after the path of our Master!

Jesus came lowly. Jesus came humble. Jesus came to serve. Jesus came in a manger. Jesus came to be worshipped by shepherds and followed by outcasts. Jesus came on a donkey. Jesus came without a home. Jesus came to a cross. How we need a new mindset when frustration stems from our lives looking a little more like His than we think they should. We aren't called to be the palace-minded who are concerned about our own comforts, but rather people-minded, concerned about the comforts of others. We aren't to be those who forget what it's like to be in the trenches with others. We aren't to be those who forget the ones who are chained in prison, chained in despair, chained in bondage, chained to sin, or chained to the past. Jesus came, mindful of the plight of others above His own, mindful of the dirty feet of others above His own, and mindful of the need of a heavenly home above the need of His earthly one. May this mind of the Servant be within us today!

"Evening and morning and at noon I will pray, and cry aloud, and He shall hear my voice."
Psalm 55:17

Magnify!
The Servant

"Jesus called them together and said, "You know that those who are regarded as rulers of the Gentiles lord it over them, and their high officials exercise authority over them. Not so with you. Instead, whoever wants to become great among you must be your servant, and whoever wants to be first must be slave of all. For even the Son of Man did not come to be served, but to serve,
and to give his life as a ransom for many."
Mark 10:42-45 (NIV)

"For you have been called to live in freedom, my brothers and sisters. But don't use your freedom to satisfy your sinful nature. Instead, use your freedom to serve one another in love. For the entire law is fulfilled in keeping this one command: Love your neighbor as yourself."
Galatians 5:13 (NLT)

"And if you will indeed obey my commandments that I command you today, to love the LORD your God, and to serve him with all your heart and with all your soul, then he will send the rains in their proper seasons—the early and late rains—so you can bring in your harvests of grain, new wine, and olive oil."
Deuteronomy 11:13-14 (ESV)

"Let no one seek his own, but each one the other's well-being."
1 Corinthians 10:24

"Servants, be obedient to them that are your masters according to the flesh, with fear and trembling, in singleness of your heart, as unto Christ; Not with eyeservice, as menpleasers; but as the servants of Christ, doing the will of God from the heart; With good will doing service,
as to the Lord, and not to men:"
Ephesians 6:5-7

"No one can serve two masters. Either you will hate the one and love the other, or you will be devoted to the one and despise the other. You cannot serve both God and money."
Matthew 6:24 (NIV)

"This, then, is how you ought to regard us: as servants of Christ and as those entrusted with the mysteries God has revealed."
1 Corinthians 4:1 (NIV)

"And if it seems evil to you to serve the LORD, choose for yourselves this day whom you will serve, whether the gods which your fathers served that were on the other side of the River, or the gods of the Amorites, in whose land you dwell. But as for me and my house, we will serve the LORD."
Joshua 24:15

"Jesus, knowing that the Father had given all things into His hands, and that He had come from God and was going to God, rose from supper and laid aside His garments, took a towel and girded Himself. After that, He poured water into a basin and began to wash the disciples' feet, and to wipe them with the towel with which He was girded. Then He came to Simon Peter. And Peter said to Him, "Lord, are You washing my feet?" Jesus answered and said to him, "What I am doing you do not understand now, but you will know after this." Peter said to Him, "You shall never wash my feet!" Jesus answered him, "If I do not wash you, you have no part with Me." Simon Peter said to Him, "Lord, not my feet only, but also my hands and my head!" Jesus said to him, "He who is bathed needs only to wash his feet, but is completely clean; and you are clean, but not all of you." For He knew who would betray Him; therefore He said, "You are not all clean." So when He had washed their feet, taken His garments, and sat down again, He said to them, "Do you know what I have done to you? You call Me Teacher and Lord, and you say well, for so I am. If I then, your Lord and Teacher, have washed your feet, you also ought to wash one another's feet. For I have given you an example, that you should do as I have done to you. Most assuredly, I say to you, a servant is not greater than his master; nor is he who is sent greater than he who sent him. If you know these things, blessed are you if you do them."
John 13:3-17

> "Enter into His gates with thanksgiving, and into His courts with praise. Be thankful to Him, and bless His name. For the LORD is good; His mercy is everlasting, and His truth endures to all generations."
> Psalm 100:4-5

Thank You Jesus today for…

Day 29
Magnify!
God's Wisdom

In John 20, the disciples are locked up in a room together with troubled hearts. They've just witnessed the death of their Beloved Jesus and are living in fear over what they saw and Who they lost. But suddenly Jesus rushes in with them, declaring His peace to them, breathing His breath upon them, and bestowing them with the gift of the Holy Spirit. What a beautiful picture of wisdom this is! Have you ever had a troubled heart or an anxious mind over a decision that needed to be made? Have you ever stood at the crossroads of life wondering which way to go? Haven't we all? James tells us that we can ask for wisdom, and that God will pour it out upon us "liberally and without reproach." All we ever have to do is cry out in humble declaration of our need for God's wisdom, and His perfect wisdom will come abundantly upon us, with no annoyance from Him! Just like the comfort the disciples felt that day when the presence of Jesus drew near; they could feel His breath upon their troubled hearts and they had the guidance of the Holy Spirit within them, so wisdom comes upon us. Wisdom comes when we call God's Presence near us, when His breath is breathed upon us, and when we're listening to the Holy Spirit's guiding within us. And the result is peace.

> "Blessed be your glorious name, and may it be exalted above all blessing and praise. You alone are the LORD. You made the heavens, even the highest heavens, and all their starry host, the earth and all that is on it, the seas and all that is in them. You give life to everything, and the multitudes of heaven worship you."
> Nehemiah 9:5-6 (NIV)

Maybe you're like me and have a little drawer in your home devoted to all the manuals of everything you own. Although now, with everything online, I'm not sure why I keep them all! You can search the internet and find the manual for pretty much everything, or even better, a video of how to fix what you're trying to fix. When we don't know how to do something, how to use something, how to fix something, or what is wrong with something, in one way or another we reach out to the ones who created the product because they know more than we do about how to use what it is that they created. Nehemiah declares praise over the One who is the Creator, sustainer, and life-Giver of everything. With God being the Creator of all, who would know greater than Him how to do something, what needs to be done, and when to do it? When I couldn't figure out why my vacuum cleaner wasn't working, I looked online for trouble-shooting videos and I trusted what they said. Why? Because the people who made the vacuum cleaner obviously know more about it than I do! As the Creator of the heavens and the earth, why wouldn't I trust His wisdom regarding my life? As the One who gives life to everything that there is, why wouldn't I look to Him for wisdom on how to live my life? As the One who created me for His good pleasure, why wouldn't I live in the way that He calls me to live? I've heard of wisdom described as "knowledge applied." When we have the knowledge that God is the Creator of everything and the life-Giver of all, I think the applied wisdom of that knowledge would be for us to let Him be in charge of everything we do! Sometimes things get so broken that following a video on the internet isn't even going to help us. That's when we take what we have to someone who won't just tell us how to do it, but will take it and fix it for us. We trust their wisdom to fix it. When we take our lives and place them into the loving hands of the One who created us, this is exactly what we're doing! We're saying, "You know more. You fix this. You heal this. You do this. I'll trust what You know above my own limited knowledge!"

There's a little story that I love in the book of Acts. Revival is bursting forth in Jerusalem, and Philip is right in the middle of it all. Suddenly God calls him to go to the desert, seemingly out in the middle of nowhere. Out in the wilderness, Philip finds a eunuch who is sitting in his chariot, reading the book of Isaiah and wondering what it means. Philip runs over to the chariot and is able to explain to this man the message of salvation from Isaiah. This Ethiopian eunuch gives his life to Jesus right then and there and gets baptized in water that God just seems to place in the middle of the desert just for him, just for this moment. Church history records that this Ethiopian eunuch went home to Ethiopia with the message of Jesus, and a great revival spread throughout his country! In the middle of an area on the map that is mostly Muslim, Ethiopia still stands as a predominantly Christian nation today. This is just the way the wisdom of God seems to work! Usually His directives don't seem to make practical sense, and often they seem to call us to the opposite direction of what we think should be done. Usually we wonder what God is doing because we can't see the whole picture, and the evidence that we made a right choice doesn't always spring up right away. Yet there are abundant blessings found in every right decision, as we choose to follow the wisdom of the One who gave us life. His ways are high above ours. We can't expect to be able to understand them, and they won't always make sense to us. He knows more than we do, and that's precisely why we can run to Him for wisdom and guidance. We can trust ourselves to the One whose ways are high above our own and seek His abundant wisdom for every moment He calls us to live today!

"Evening and morning and at noon I will pray, and cry aloud, and He shall hear my voice."
Psalm 55:17

Magnify!
God's Wisdom

"If you need wisdom, ask our generous God, and he will give it to you. He will not rebuke you for asking. But when you ask him, be sure that your faith is in God alone. Do not waver, for a person with divided loyalty is as unsettled as a wave of the sea that is blown and tossed by the wind. Such people should not expect to receive anything from the Lord. Their loyalty is divided between God and the world, and they are unstable in everything they do."
James 1:5-8 (NLT)

"For jealousy and selfishness are not God's kind of wisdom. Such things are earthly, unspiritual, and demonic. For wherever there is jealousy and selfish ambition, there you will find disorder and evil of every kind. But the wisdom from above is first of all pure. It is also peace loving, gentle at all times, and willing to yield to others. It is full of mercy and the fruit of good deeds. It shows no favoritism and is always sincere."
James 3:15-17 (NLT)

"For the LORD grants wisdom!
From his mouth come knowledge and understanding.
He grants a treasure of common sense to the honest."
Proverbs 2:6-7 (NLT)

"Oh, how great are God's riches and wisdom and knowledge! How impossible it is for us to understand his decisions and his ways! For who can know the LORD's thoughts? Who knows enough to give him advice? And who has given him so much that he needs to pay it back? For everything comes from him and exists by his power and is intended for his glory. All glory to him forever! Amen."
Romans 11:33-36 (NLT)

"Before the mountains were born, before you gave birth to the earth and the world, from beginning to end, you are God."
Psalm 90:2 (NLT)

"In the beginning was the Word, and the Word was with God, and the Word was God. He was with God in the beginning. Through him all things were made; without him nothing was made that has been made. In him was life, and that life was the light of all mankind."
John 1:1-4 (NIV)

"The LORD wraps himself in light as with a garment; He stretches out the heavens like a tent and lays the beams of his upper chambers on their waters.
He makes the clouds his chariot and rides on the wings of the wind.
He makes winds his messengers, flames of fire his servants.
He set the earth on its foundations; it can never be moved.
You covered it with the watery depths as with a garment; the waters stood above the mountains. But at your rebuke the waters fled, at the sound of your thunder they took to flight;
they flowed over the mountains,
they went down into the valleys, to the place you assigned for them.
You set a boundary they cannot cross;
never again will they cover the earth.
He makes springs pour water into the ravines;
it flows between the mountains.
They give water to all the beasts of the field;
the wild donkeys quench their thirst.
The birds of the sky nest by the waters; they sing among the branches.
He waters the mountains from his upper chambers; the land is satisfied by the fruit of his work. He makes grass grow for the cattle,
and plants for people to cultivate—
bringing forth food from the earth: wine that gladdens human hearts, oil to make their faces shine, and bread that sustains their hearts. The trees of the LORD are well watered, the cedars of Lebanon that he planted. There the birds make their nests; the stork has its home in the junipers. The high mountains belong to the wild goats; the crags are a refuge for the hyrax. He made the moon to mark the seasons,
and the sun knows when to go down.
You bring darkness, it becomes night,
and all the beasts of the forest prowl. The lions roar for their prey and seek their food from God. The sun rises, and they steal away; they return and lie down in their dens. Then people go out to their work,
to their labor until evening.
How many are Your works, LORD! In wisdom
you made them all;
the earth is full of Your creatures."
Psalm 104:2-24 (NIV)

*"Enter into His gates with thanksgiving, and into His courts with praise. Be thankful to Him, and bless His name.
For the LORD is good; His mercy is everlasting, and His truth endures to all generations."*
Psalm 100:4-5

Thank You Jesus today for…

Day 30
Magnify!
His Strength

Our perception of strength is usually dependent upon a weakness displayed in contrast. I can say that my muscles are tremendously huge, and that I'm one of the strongest people around- but in reality, that's only true when I'm standing in a room full of toddlers and there are no other adults available for a muscle-and-strength comparison! I look really strong compared to a three-year-old, but so very weak and flabby compared to someone who loves to go to the gym and pump iron every day! Our version of strength is always measured by the weakness of another. Samson was considered to be strong because he could carry things with endurance and strength that no other human of his time had. A body builder is considered to be strong because they can lift weights that an average untrained human can't lift. The wind is described as being strong when it's blowing harder than usual. We say we have strong feelings about something when we have a greater emotional attachment than usual. But the strength of God is not the average perception of strength that comes from comparison alone. God's strength doesn't look stronger simply because it's measured against human weakness. His strength actually *IS* stronger than any earthly strength can be, greater than any earthly strength that can be experienced, and mightier than any earthly strength that could ever be displayed by the strongest earthly strength we know.

> "Have you never heard? Have you never understood?
> The LORD is the everlasting God, the Creator of all the earth.
> He never grows weak or weary. No one can measure the depths of his understanding. He gives power to the weak and strength to the powerless. Even youths will become weak and tired, and young men will fall in exhaustion. But those who trust in the LORD will find new strength. They will soar high on wings like eagles. They will run and not grow weary. They will walk and not faint."
> Isaiah 40:28-31 (NLT)

The strongest earthly strength has limitations, weakness, and a breaking point. Even the strongest people have moments where they're too weary, too tired, with no more strength left in them for the moment. God's strength isn't strong because it's measured against our humanity. His strength is *endless*! It doesn't wear out, give out, fade, falter, or fail the way that ours does. He's not strong for just a season before His strength diminishes. God's strength never runs out and is never less-than. It's in

His strength that He lifts us up, enabling us to leap over walls, to climb the high hills, to fight the enemy until our dying day, to resist temptation and sin, to continue to love the difficult, and to just be absolutely covered by His strength in thousands of different moments each day. His strength gives us the ability to sing when we're broken, to feel His nearness when we're crushed, and to be filled with joy in hard times because His joy *IS* our strength. Strength is also thought of as the ability to weather a tragedy with great endurance, and sometimes God's strength upon us just gives us the ability to keep on going. Strength in a marathon could be thought of partially as muscles and ability, but also as the tenacity to simply keep choosing to press on toward the mark. Psalm 84 portrays us as going from "strength to strength" when describing the endurance that it takes to carry out our pilgrimage here on earth. Isaiah describes God as, "our strength and our song," as He becomes our salvation. He removes all fear by the very strength of His Presence within us. God shows His strength to us needy ones by giving His strength as our refuge, His strength as our fortress, and His strength as our mighty strong tower that we can run to in times of need. There is no other strength that can penetrate or topple His strength within our lives when we are looking to Him and leaning upon Him with all that we are.

Paul describes God's strength as being strongest throughout our times of weakness, because when we reach our weakest moment, we finally cry out for the full strength of God. When we're completely depleted of our own resources is when we become the strongest because we choose to decrease so that God can increase through us. His strength is displayed greatest through our weakness, not just because He's stronger, but because there is more of Him and less of us in the moment. Being filled with the strength of God is not a "rise up" moment of muscular Christians. It's a depletion of our own selves, our own resources, and our own self-reliance, knowing that we can do all things through Christ who strengthens us and absolutely nothing worthwhile on our own. It's a depletion of all the abilities we think we bring to the table so that we can trade our puny strength for His mighty, powerful, awesome strength that does not wear out, grow weary, faint, fail, or fall.

Is there a great trade of strength that needs to take place somewhere today? Is there an area that you have been trying to run through in your own faltering strength, rather than God's? Like a little toddler trying to wrestle his daddy, our own strength is just simply not enough. Let's stop wrestling and instead climb on our strong God's back today, to be carried by His endless, enduring strength.

"Evening and morning and at noon I will pray, and cry aloud, and He shall hear my voice."
Psalm 55:17

Magnify!
His Strength

"The LORD is my light and my salvation; Whom shall I fear? The LORD is the strength of my life; Of whom shall I be afraid?"
Psalm 27:1

"For I can do everything through Christ, who gives me strength."
Philippians 4:13 (NLT)

"But the salvation of the righteous is from the LORD; He is their strength in the time of trouble."
Psalm 37:39

"This is a sacred day before our Lord. Don't be dejected and sad, for the joy of the LORD is your strength!"
Nehemiah 8:10 (NLT)

"O LORD, our Lord, how majestic is your name in all the earth, who have displayed your splendor above the heavens! From the mouth of infants and nursing babes you have established strength because of your adversaries, to make the enemy and the revengeful cease."
Psalm 8:1-2 (NASB)

"Seek the LORD and His strength; Seek His face evermore! Remember His marvelous works which He has done, His wonders, and the judgments of His mouth"
1 Chronicles 16:11-12

"The LORD is my strength and shield. I trust him with all my heart. He helps me, and my heart is filled with joy. I burst out in songs of thanksgiving. The LORD gives his people strength. He is a safe fortress for his anointed king."
Psalm 28:7-8 (NLT)

"I love you, LORD; you are my strength.
The LORD is my rock, my fortress, and my savior;
my God is my rock, in whom I find protection.
He is my shield, the power that saves me,
and my place of safety... God arms me with strength,
and he makes my way perfect."
Psalm 18:1-2, 32 (NLT)

"The LORD is my strength and my song; he has given me victory.
This is my God, and I will praise him— my father's God,
and I will exalt him!
The LORD is a warrior; Yahweh is his name!...
Your right hand, O LORD, is glorious in power.
Your right hand, O LORD, smashes the enemy.
In the greatness of your majesty,
you overthrow those who rise against you."
Exodus 15:2-3, 6-7 (NLT)

"Blessed are You, LORD God of Israel, our Father, forever and ever.
Yours, O LORD, is the greatness, the power and the glory,
the victory and the majesty; for all that is in heaven and in earth is Yours;
Yours is the kingdom, O LORD, And You are exalted as head over all.
Both riches and honor come from You, and You reign over all.
In Your hand is power and might; In Your hand it is to make great
And to give strength to all."
1 Chronicles 29:10-12

"Let the words of my mouth and the meditation of my heart Be
acceptable in Your sight, O LORD, my strength and my Redeemer."
Psalm 19:14

"The LORD is my rock and my fortress and my deliverer;
The God of my strength, in whom I will trust;
My shield and the horn of my salvation,
My stronghold and my refuge;
My Savior, You save me from violence.
I will call upon the LORD, who is worthy to be praised;
So shall I be saved from my enemies."
2 Samuel 22:2-4

"The Sovereign LORD is my strength! He makes me
as surefooted as a deer,
able to tread upon the heights."
Habakkuk 3:19 (NLT)

> *"Enter into His gates with thanksgiving, and into His courts with praise. Be thankful to Him, and bless His name. For the LORD is good; His mercy is everlasting, and His truth endures to all generations."*
> Psalm 100:4-5

Thank You Jesus today for…

Beautiful friend...

I pray that you found such grace, peace, joy, satisfaction, and rich fulfillment in this place of intentional prayer. I pray that God has moved and worked mightily in and through your life during these thirty days. I pray that He has removed obstacles, brought about salvation, healed relationships, restored the broken places, and given great victories through your places of prayer. I pray that you are filled with a greater wonder and sense of awe toward your God than you were when you began this journey. I pray that God met you in such powerful ways; answering your prayers, calling you to higher places, and charging your heart up with encouragement for the glorious duty of battling on behalf of God's Kingdom through prayer.

May God infuse your heart with great joy as you continue to kneel before Him daily, interceding on behalf of those people and situations that He brings near to your heart. May He continue setting your eyes upon the heavenly realm as this earth grows more and more dim to your sight. May God continue to be more greatly magnified to your soul each day, as you remind your heart of His vast beauty, faithfulness, and steadfast love. May you continue to choose to magnify His glorious attributes above all that this world holds dear.

May God continue to turn your heart and gaze upward toward Him. He is the all-glorious God, and He is the most deserving of our attention, praise, and adoration each day. I pray that He continues to capture your heart in a greater way, day after day, until the day He finally calls you home, and your magnified faith becomes your magnified reality.

God bless you, precious one.

> **"Oh, magnify the LORD with me,**
> **and let us exalt His name together."**
> **Psalm 34:3**

Made in the USA
Columbia, SC
22 November 2022